Clavichord for Beginners

Joan Benson, 1982

PUBLICATIONS OF THE EARLY MUSIC INSTITUTE
Paul Elliott, editor

Clavichord
for
Beginners

Joan Benson

INDIANA UNIVERSITY PRESS

Bloomington & Indianapolis

This book is a publication of

INDIANA UNIVERSITY PRESS
Office of Scholarly Publishing
Herman B Wells Library 350
1320 East 10th Street
Bloomington, Indiana 47405 USA

iupress.indiana.edu

Telephone   800-842-6796
Fax   812-855-7931

Manufactured in the United States of America

Library of Congress Cataloging-in-Publication Data

Benson, Joan, author.
Clavichord for beginners / Joan Benson.
pages cm. — (Publications of the Early Music Institute)
Includes bibliographical references.
ISBN 978-0-253-01158-9 (paperback) — ISBN 978-0-253-01164-0 (ebook)
1. Clavichord—Methods. 2. Clavichord music—Instruction and study.
I. Title. II. Series: Publications of the Early Music Institute.
MT252.B46 2014
786.3'193—dc23
2013042017

1 2 3 4 5   19 18 17 16 15 14

I dedicate this book to Buddhist masters who have taught me to see each moment as a fresh beginning.

Contents

Preface and Acknowledgments

SEVERAL SUMMERS AGO Wendy Gillespie, the esteemed early music specialist, visited my home in Eugene, Oregon. As we strolled along a woodland path, she asked what I, in my eighties, still wished to accomplish with the clavichord. I responded that I hoped to find a way to encourage others to enjoy this exquisite instrument. Since clavichord teachers are rare today, we envisioned a book of exercises so simple that a beginner might start the clavichord without a personal instructor. Thus this manual, combined with a master class DVD, was born.

This book is for all clavichord beginners, including amateurs and professional keyboardists. It is for those who wish to experience the quieting effect of this delicate instrument. Special exercises and lessons are meant to stimulate sensitivity to touch and tone that can affect all keyboard playing. The intention is to show the way to express subtle feelings and perceptions on the clavichord, infusing the softest pianissimo with a vitality of its own.

Today the beginning clavichordist is lucky to have access to six centuries of clavichords, including various styles of construction, repertoire, and playing techniques. Copies of original treatises and music manuscripts are available, and copies of all kinds of antique clavichords are for sale. A clavichord beginner may explore historical evidence and see how it is—and might be—applied.

Antique clavichords have changed and been altered, however, and the finest research can only hint at how music originally sounded. In fact, "early" music ideally was improvisational, reflecting the moment. Thus, this manual is not intended to freeze sounds into imitations or oblige the student to play in one set way. Rather, it is meant to open new vistas for the clavichord beginner, offering a fresh sense of musical meaning, expression, and spontaneity.

I myself am grateful for the unusual opportunity of studying with some of Europe's finest keyboard teachers and performers born about a century ago. I thank Macario Santiago Kastner of Lisbon and Fritz Neumeyer of Freiburg for so generously sharing their expertise in clavichord playing and their knowledge of early music. Frau Alfred Kreutz, widow of the once-famed German clavichordist, confirmed my own ideas on dynamic shading. Through Viola Thern of Vienna I belatedly acquired finger independence at the keyboard. Above all, I am grateful to the great Swiss pianist Edwin Fischer for his profound musical insights, his beautiful singing sound, and his inspiring encouragement of my own artistry.

Regarding this entire project, I am indebted to all those who gave so freely of both time and expertise. I particularly thank Professor Wendy Gillespie, Professor Thomas Mathiesen, Sung Lee, and the Early Music Institute for initiating and helping to back the project.

For the book itself, I am deeply grateful to Professor Marita McClymonds whose consistent and caring critique of my work helped to propel it towards completion. Likewise, I am grateful to Dr. Raymond Morse for his many hours of excellent consultation. I thank Professor William Mahrt, Professor Sandra Soderlund, Professor Chris Chafe, Dr. Timothy Tikker, Irene Shreier-Scott, Jeff Muiderman, Edith Maddron, and photographer Donna Gilhousen, In addition, I thank the University of Oregon's music and research librarians, the Smithsonian Institution Archives, and the kind permission of Nederlands Muziek Instituut to use the original edition of Method pieces by Francesco Pasquale Ricci. I also greatly appreciate the interest of piano artists András Schiff and Paul Badura-Skoda.

With the CD, I am grateful to Grammy-winner Barry Phillips for his dedication to its production and restoration. I thank John Nunes for his part in the production, and I greatly appreciate the expert transfers of tapes and LPs made by him and by Eric Jacobs of Audio Archives. In addition, I thank Jay Kadis, Bill Levey, Art Maddox, and Jenalabs for their gracious assistance.

For the DVD, I thank John Winninger for his video and for his kind cooperation with its final editing. Likewise, I am grateful to Carolyn Horn and Theresa Hughes for their generous participation.

Clavichord for Beginners

CHAPTER ONE

Clavichord for All Keyboardists

> At least in the beginning, the clavichord is unquestionably best suit-
> ed for learning, for on no other keyboard instrument is it possible to
> achieve finesse in playing as well as on this one.
>
> Daniel Gottlob Türk, *School of Clavier Playing* (*Klavierschule,* 1789)

What Is a Clavichord?

A good clavichord is the simplest, softest, and most sensitively responsive of all keyboard instruments. Its basic structure is as follows:

An oblong wooden frame contains a soundboard on the right. Attached to it are
one to three bridges on which strings are stretched. These strings extend from tuning
pins on the far right to hitch pins on the far left. Below and perpendicular to the
strings are wooden key levers balanced on pins. When a finger presses down the key
end of a lever, the opposite end of the lever automatically rises. Protruding upward
from this far end is a metal tangent, which strikes and presses against a pair or triplet
of strings. These strings vibrate from tangent to bridge, creating both tone and pitch.
To the left of the tangents, cloth strips (listing) are woven among the strings. They
block extraneous sound that might come from the left of each tangent and stop a
tone when the key and its tangent are released.

The clavichord is the only keyboard instrument on which a tone can be altered
as long as it lasts. The initial dynamic level is determined by the strength, speed, and
distance of the tangent's (and finger's) attack. While the tangent stays in contact with
the string, the sound will bloom and then gradually fade. During that time any fluctuation in finger and tangent pressure will change the pitch and carrying power of
the tone. By varying this pressure purposely once (a *portato*) or a number of times (a
Bebung), the performer can produce special effects of great delicacy. The relationship
of finger to string offers dynamic and articulative subtleties, some so small they can
scarcely be perceived.

The clavichord is a very personal instrument, heard most directly by the player.
It is able to reflect, inspire, and deepen a player's entire being.

FIGURE 1.1 Clavichord, c. 1800. *Photograph courtesy of Donna Gilhousen.*

Clavichord for Keyboard Beginners

The earlier one begins to play the clavichord, the further one may progress . . . with regard to dexterity. For at the tenderest age, the fingers are still supple.

Daniel Gottlob Türk, *School of Clavier Playing*

In former centuries a child often began music lessons on the clavichord. The instrument was small and easily portable, the keys were short, the touch and tone were light. A child learned to listen to tones and to keep a steady pitch. Practicing did not disturb others, and little maintenance was required beyond tuning. Today the word "keyboard" usually refers to the computer. Video games, amplified sounds, and hectic schedules keep many children from having the tranquility in which to dream. The expressive clavichord can be the perfect outlet for a sensitive child.

The clavichord is excellent for an adult keyboard beginner for the same reasons. Unlike the synthesizer, it stimulates a sensitivity to touch and sound. By minimizing arm weight, it builds finger awareness and a delicacy of tonal control. Above all, in this high-strung world, it can offer a quiet space for privacy, clarity, and repose.

For Harpsichordists

The clavichord is excellent for novices "to train their hands on the keyboard so that they may later play with more confidence and suppleness on the harpsichord."

Pierre Trichet, *Traité des instruments de musique* (c. 1640),
quoted in Brauchli, *The Clavichord*

A good clavichordist makes an accomplished harpsichordist, but not the reverse. The clavichord is needed for the study of good performance, and the harpsichord to develop proper finger strength. . . .

Those who concentrate on the harpsichord grow accustomed to playing in only one color. The varied touch which the competent clavichordist brings to the harpsichord remains hidden from them.

C. P. E. Bach, *Essay on the True Art of Playing Keyboard Instruments*

Bach's way of playing would not have been devised at all without the clavichord. . . . He who once masters this instrument plays the harpsichord quite differently from those who never touch a clavichord.

Johann Friedrich Reichardt, *Briefe eines aufmerksamen Reisenden* (1774)

It was customary in earlier periods for a keyboardist to play both the harpsichord and the clavichord. Even today, each has its place. The brilliant harpsichord is a more highly articulate solo and ensemble instrument. When a key is depressed, the pluck of a plectrum makes a string vibrate. When the key is released, a damper blocks the sound.

A harpsichordist can control only the beginning and ending of each tone. Dynamic variations are made by differences in musical textures, articulation, and instrumental resonance. On some harpsichords, a player can couple or uncouple separate sets of strings, offering contrasting timbres or levels of pitch.

The more intimate clavichord has much to offer the harpsichordist. It encourages the player to follow a tone as it blooms and fades. The clavichord's soft and flexible sounds can attune the harpsichordist to fine details and the interrelationship of voices. Fingers and ears learn to form those infinitesimal threads of expression that enhance a musician's performance.

For Players of Early Pianos

A clavichord is better than a harpsichord or a pianoforte for the beginner. . . . Anyone who learns from one of the latter instruments will never be as refined in playing and in expression as a person who receives beginning instruction on the clavichord.

Georg Simon Löhlein, *Clavier-Schule* (1765),
translated in Sandra Soderlund, *How Did They Play?*

The eighteenth-century clavichord and early piano have much in common.[1] Both represent a fresh approach to music that expands the dynamic variations of tones. Particularly with large, five-octave clavichords and their long-lasting tones, crescendos and diminuendos can be extended over measures, and quick changes of dynamics can be dramatic. Instrument makers in late eighteenth-century Sweden went so far as to specialize in color-rich clavichords containing huge soundboards and compasses of up to six octaves.

In the case of the early piano, small leather-covered hammers strike the strings to produce sounds, which are then silenced by cloth or leather dampers. As with clavichords, the sound will vary in loudness according to initial finger attack and pressure. Unlike clavichordists, however, early pianists can relax this pressure after the initial attack, since only the beginning and ending of notes are controlled. Still, the early piano's hammer power, una corda, and sustaining mechanisms can affect the quality, loudness, and length of sound. In general, by studying the clavichord, players can become more sensitized to the subtle dynamics and articulations available on different eighteenth-century pianos, ranging from Cristofori copies to English grands.

The link between the clavichord and early piano is particularly apparent in Germany and Austria. C. P. E. Bach (from here on called Emanuel), Haydn, and Mozart played the clavichord as children and remained clavichordists all their lives. The sensitive touch they learned on the clavichord they naturally applied to the early piano.

It was common in these countries for keyboard makers to build both clavichords and early pianos. Some of the earliest pianos, by Gottlieb Silbermann, were sold to King Frederick the Great while Emanuel Bach served in his court. Probably the same Silbermann also produced the famous clavichord that Bach owned and played. Its astounding dynamic range allowed him to express a breathtaking scope of emotions.

The sensitive, light, clear "Viennese" fortepianos that Haydn and Mozart played respond completely to a clavichord touch. Thus, I advise those who want to make music on such early pianos to begin with the clavichord.

I first discovered the close connection between clavichords and "Viennese" fortepianos in a European museum in the 1960s.[2] While preparing for a clavichord concert, I was locked in the hall overnight by mistake. To while away the hours, I turned to three elegant fortepianos placed on a platform. I opened the lid of one by Andreas Stein and began to play. Exquisite tones filled the hall, and I listened, amazed. Then I played a Nanette Streicher fortepiano and one made by Anton Walter. My clavichord approach seemed to suit these instruments precisely. Time passed unnoticed, and I was completely carried away. This experience inspired me to feature early pianos along with the clavichord in later performances.

For Modern Pianists

During the time of Mendelssohn, Chopin, Schumann, and Liszt, pianos continued to change. Yet at best their shallow key dips, light, sensitive, and rapid actions, and great capacity for colors were naturally attuned to the emotional, melismatic lines of Chopin and the luxurious orchestral effects of Liszt.

This colorful and pliable palette, coupled with a warm, full sound, is found in iron-framed modern pianos of the early twentieth century. The Schubert Club in Saint Paul, Minnesota, owns a stunning 1908 American Steinway Model B. When visiting concert pianists encounter this instrument, they are tempted to overdrive its fragile action. Yet as a clavichordist, I found this piano highly expressive and rewarding to play.

In 1901 the American pianist William Mason, who advocated arm weight coupled with relaxation, described a piano technique that recalls that of the clavichord.

To produce a soft tone, fingertips are pulled inward toward the palm. "Through the medium of this touch," Mason wrote, "pianissimo effects are possible which no other mechanism can reach; for passages of the most extreme delicacy and softness still retain the quality of vitality and clearness of outline."[3]

In our current era, dominated by loud, bold sounds, all pianists, both professionals and amateurs, can profit from playing the clavichord. The detailed finger control and auditory acuity it develops can enhance and expand interpretative and technical skills. Two twentieth-century piano artists who owned and played clavichords are Claudio Arrau (grand-pupil of Liszt) and tiny-fingered Mieczysław Horszowski (great-grand-pupil of Beethoven and Chopin). In the twenty-first century, András Schiff reflects the clavichord in his piano performances of keyboard music by Johann Sebastian Bach.

Through the clavichord, pianists are encouraged to go far beyond *piano* and *forte* to a finer range of dynamics. They will discover they can shade Bach's music and clarify the interaction of each voice in a fugue. A melisma of Chopin will become intricately tapered like a vocal improvisation. Lowering the key slightly before beginning to make a softer tone will be useful in the impressionistic music of Debussy.

For a millennium music festival in 2000, I performed on the modern piano for the first time in forty years. It seemed natural, once again, to use arm weight and the una corda and damper pedals and to include the hall's reflection of sound. The ease with which I conveyed the languid, misty shadings of John Cage's *Landscape #3* I attribute to the clavichord.

For Organists

> First take the clavichord . . . because what you will have learned on the clavichord you will then be able to play easily and well on the organ.
>
> Sebastian Virdung, *Musica getutscht und ausgezogen* (1511),
> quoted in Brauchli, *The Clavichord*

Traditionally, organists valued the clavichord because it gave them the option of practicing and composing at home. Thus, they avoided both the unpleasantness of working in a cold church and the expense of hiring a bellows operator. Famous performers on both instruments included Burgundy's Henri Bredemers (1472–1522), Spain's Antonio de Cabezón (1510–66), and Johann Sebastian Bach and his son Wilhelm Friedemann.

The organ differs from other keyboard instruments in that its loud, layered tones remain fully sustained until released. Most pipes are far from the player, and music continues to reverberate throughout the entire hall, which functions as part of the instrument. By playing organ music on the clavichord, the player can acquire a light, more articulate touch. By hearing the sound up close, the organist can focus on a clearly defined miniature version of the music.

Pedal clavichords existed as early as the fifteenth century. An eighteenth-century example by Johann David Gerstenberg survives in Leipzig's Museum of Musical Instruments. This instrument consists of two clavichords, one above the other, resting on a third clavichord that contains key levers controlled by pedals. The mechanism is so sensitive that it encourages finesse in pedal technique. In fact, it was said of J. S. Bach that he "ran over the pedals . . . as if his feet had wings."[4]

Clavichord skills prove valuable indeed when dealing with historical organs and their modern copies. The connection is particularly clear in the case of specific instruments of the sixteenth century. In fact, decades ago in Brescia I had the opportunity to spend days playing an organ in the church of San Giuseppe. This exquisite organ, completed by Graziadio Antegnati in 1581, is very responsive to a clavichordist's touch. With its twelve stops, low wind pressure, shallow key dip, and pull-down pedals, this instrument offers a trace of shading, since fingers and feet control how the pipe valves open and close. In fact, the remarkable blending of sounds and the balanced, unifying effect of the entire organ recall to mind my favorite sixteenth-century clavichord, which is likely of Italian origin.

This "Clavichord #3" resides in Leipzig's Museum of Musical Instruments. Highly fretted (with multiple tangents striking a single pair of strings), it has three bridges and nineteen pairs of strings of equal length. One soundboard runs under the key levers, and a second lies higher to the right. The instrument has a compass of four octaves, with a short octave in the bass. This small, narrow clavichord is unusually sensitive to subtleties of dynamics and articulation. Exquisitely made, its thin walls are protected by an outer wooden case. It is amazing how far the instrument's delicate, pure tones can carry throughout adjacent rooms.

Both the clavichord in Leipzig and the organ in Brescia show the consummate craftsmanship of the period when they were made. Both number among the most beautiful keyboard instruments I have ever heard or played.

For Singing Clavichordists

> Above all, lose no opportunity to hear artistic singing. In so doing, the keyboardist will learn to think in terms of song. Indeed, it is a good practice to sing instrumental melodies in order to reach an understanding of their correct performance.
>
> C. P. E. Bach, *Essay on the True Art of Playing Keyboard Instruments*

In earlier times, musicians customarily sang to the clavichord as though to an intimate friend. In this way, they might share the joys and pains of love or find relief from loneliness and worry. Singing and playing sacred music so softly also encouraged a special closeness with God.

Mid-fifteenth-century carvings depict angels singing with the clavichord as a symbol for celestial music. Much later, two collections of C. P. E. Bach's sacred songs (1780 and 1786) gained immediate success, particularly among German Pietists. The passionate words came from the pen of Emanuel's close friend, Christoph Christian Sturm, the controversial minister of Saint Peter's Church in Hamburg. (Beethoven was deeply affected by a copy of Sturm's *Reflections on the Works of God in Nature*.)

In the 1970s a young, pure-voiced soprano and I performed several of C. P. E. Bach's songs.[5] To sing with the clavichord, she purposely softened her clear voice.

Rather than project sounds toward the audience, she simply sat in a chair, looking down at the printed page. Her tenderly plaintive "Jesus in Gethsemane" and "Über die Finsternis Kurz vor dem Tode Jesu" expressed with quiet passion Christ's final hours.

Singing one voice in a musical texture creates an awareness of its shape and how it interacts with the shapes of other voices. When preparing for a concert, I liked to sing one part at a time, playing the other parts on the clavichord. While practicing this way in Bali, Indonesia, I became aware of hushed listeners in the empty hall. After the rehearsal was over, I asked why they were so attentive to simple practice. One answered, "We like to hear your voice and the way it blends with the clavichord."

More recently, when practicing a Lou Harrison keyboard sonata on the clavichord, I found myself singing wordlessly a middle movement melody in a haunting Chinese manner. "Oh, sing that way in the concert!" a friend said. I did so, which delighted the composer, who was present in the audience.

A Personal Note for Aspiring Clavichordists

In our times, the clavichord can offer a peace of mind that is difficult to find. This is particularly true when a player does not need to focus on competitiveness or technical display. As you work through the lessons in this book, the instrument's nature will gradually become comfortable for you. A sense of confidence and enjoyment will unfold as you become immersed in clavichord music itself.

CHAPTER TWO

Preparing to Play

Ways of Relaxing

In order to play the clavichord, make certain that your hands, wrists, arms, and shoulders remain flexible and at ease. The following relaxation exercises are helpful particularly before and after short practice periods.

1. Drop your arms loosely to your sides and shake them rapidly from the shoulders (like a cascading waterfall).
2. Raise your right forearm as high as your elbow. Let your hand go limp from the wrist and twirl it first clockwise and then counterclockwise.
   - Twirl your left hand in the same way.
   - Now twirl both hands in contrary motion.
   - Drop your arms and shake them.
3. Raise your arms straight out in front of you. Rotate your forearms from the elbows in contrary motion, keeping your hands and wrists relaxed.
4. Now rotate both arms from the shoulders first in one direction and then in the other in an easy, open way.

If convenient, learn a form of Qigong. These Chinese exercises can energize your body and free it from tension.[1]

Touch Awareness

The key to all clavichord playing lies in the sensitive relationship between touch and tone.

1. With your eyes closed, feel an object with your fingertips. Touch your earlobe, your clothing, or the bark of a tree. Notice the subtle variations in textures and sounds.
2. Move slowly around a room with your eyes closed. Notice how you depend on touch and sound to find your way.

Finger Awareness, Seated

1. Place the back of your right hand flat on a table, palm facing upward.
2. Slowly and easily raise your index finger. Then let it descend.
   - Attempt to keep your other fingers from moving or trembling.
   - If necessary, hold them down with the opposite hand.
3. Now lift and lower the other fingers of the right hand one at a time.
4. Repeat with the left hand. Always move in a comfortable way.

Finger Interaction, Seated

1. Bring your hands together in prayer form.
2. Cup them so that only your wrists, thumbs, and fingertips are touching.
3. Gently and repeatedly move the entire index fingers back and forth while keeping your other fingers still (figure 2.1).

FIGURE 2.1

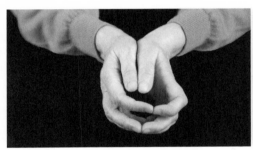

4. Similarly, move your third fingers back and forth, then your fourth fingers, and finally your fifth fingers.
5. Finally, move your two touching thumbs back and forth within the arch of your hands (figure 2.2).

FIGURE 2.2

FIGURE 2.3

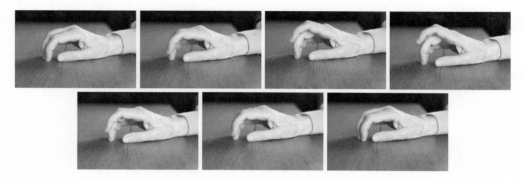

Exercise for Finger Independence

1. Place your right hand and wrist on a table in playing position with your curved fingertips in a straight line.
2. Lift and lower one finger at a time, repetitively and very *slowly,* while your wrist, thumb, and other fingers stay relaxed. If your finger trembles or any other finger moves unintentionally, simply notice without being concerned.
3. Pause after each lifting and lowering of a finger. Then try again.
4. Repeat the same exercise with your left hand (figure 2.3).

Exercise for Flexible Wrists

1. Place the fleshy tip of your right middle finger on a table and hold it there lightly.
2. Circle your wrist clockwise and then counterclockwise in an easy, relaxed way. Your hand and forearm will follow naturally.
3. Repeat with your left wrist (figure 2.4).

FIGURE 2.4

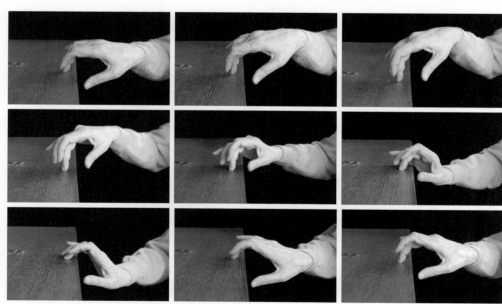

FIGURE 2.5   Joan at the clavichord, Copenhagen, 1968

Getting to Know Your Clavichord

It is important to become intimately familiar with your clavichord or clavichords. Each one differs in structure and sound. Details in playing technique depend on the instrument, its use and repertoire, and your own physical structure.

Position at the Keyboard

Sit upright in front of your clavichord, keeping your shoulders and neck relaxed. In his *Essay on the True Art of Playing Keyboard Instruments* (1753), Carl Philipp Emanuel Bach states the following:

> The performer must sit at the middle of the keyboard so that he may strike the highest as well as the lowest tones with equal ease.
>
> When the performer is in the correct position with respect to height, his forearms are suspended slightly above the fingerboard.
>
> In playing, the fingers should be arched and the muscles relaxed. . . . Stiffness hampers all movement, above all the constantly required rapid extension and contraction of the hands. . . . Those who play with flat, extended fingers suffer. . . . The fingers, because of their length, are too far removed from the thumb, which should always remain as close as possible to the hand.[2]

Control of Tone and Pitch

The clavichord is the only keyboard instrument requiring the constant adjustment of your fingers in order to produce clear sounds and stay in tune.

1. With the tip of your index finger, press down C above middle C.
   - Watch the key lever, like a seesaw, rise on the opposite end.
   - Note how the metal tangent protruding upward from the far end hits and presses against a pair of strings to produce a sound.
2. Repeat playing C with your index finger, moving it gradually from the front end of the key to the back.
   - Note that the closer your fingertip is to the front edge of the key, the more clear and controllable the sound.
3. Try playing notes from the highest to the lowest registers of the keyboard.
   - Note the differences in tone and in pressure required.
4. Push a key down so that the tangent stretches the strings too much.
   - Listen to the tone rise above pitch.

Later you will learn how to control fluctuations of pitch for special effects.

CHAPTER THREE

Clavichord Lessons, Series I

OF ALL THE major keyboard instruments, the clavichord is most like a violin. Both pitch and quality of tone are subject to your touch. The mechanism is so direct that you can actually feel your fingers, via the tangent, pressing against the strings.

Learning to play the clavichord requires focused attention. It is important to practice for short periods at first, advancing slowly. Linger for some time over each lesson, repeating it until you can apply it well. You may also consult the accompanying DVD.

Lesson One: Lowering a Key Soundlessly

1. Position yourself comfortably at the keyboard as described earlier, keeping your arms and wrists at ease.

2. Gently place all five fingertips of the right hand near the front edge of keys CDEFG an octave above middle C. (Note: You may use any five successive, natural keys for this exercise and for any suitable exercise that follows.)

3. Lower your index finger on D so slowly that you can feel the pliancy of the key's descent.

4. Watch the tangent press up against a set of strings *without making any sound.*
   - Rest there, keeping this pressure constant until the key is released.
   - Your other fingers stay quietly on the surface of their keys without your lowering them at all.

5. Try this exercise with the other fingers of your right hand, one at a time.

6. Repeat the exercise with your left hand, placing five fingers on CDEFG below middle C and starting with the index finger pressing F.

This exercise requires great patience. Only gradually will one finger function independently while the other fingers remain still. If your playing finger trembles or makes a slight sound, just observe this without concern.

Lesson Two: Making a Sound

Producing a pleasant sound may take practice . . . and can surprise you when it first occurs.

1. Place your curved right-hand fingers near the edge of CDEFG an octave above middle C.
   - Keep your thumbtip as nearly in line with the other fingertips as is comfortable.
   - All your nonplaying fingers should stay quietly on key surfaces without depressing them in the least.
2. To make a sound, lower your index finger on D, causing the tangent to strike the strings (example 3.1).

EXAMPLE 3.1

   - Note the tactile relationship between the tangent, the key, and the fleshy part of your fingertip.
3. Hold D down steadily, keeping the pressure of the tangent constant. The slightest fluctuation will change the pitch.
   - Listen to the entire length of the sound and how it fades away.
4. Release D, staying in contact with the key as it returns to rest position.
   - Cloth strips woven among the strings left of the tangent will dampen extraneous string sound.
   - The strings may buzz if the tangent is released with hesitation, especially if its surface is worn or slants incorrectly. In that case, the surface should be expertly filed.
5. Slowly repeat this exercise with your other fingers, one at a time. Remember to keep nonplaying fingers quiet and your wrist and arm at ease (example 3.2).

EXAMPLE 3.2

6. Do the same exercise with your left hand over CDEFG below middle C. First play and then repeat F with the index finger (example 3.3).

EXAMPLE 3.3

7. Then play the exercise with fingers 3, 4, 5, and 1 of the left hand, one finger at a time (example 3.4).

EXAMPLE 3.4

8. Whenever you need to rest completely, drop your hands and arms to your sides.

Lesson Three: Playing Two Notes in a Row

The way one finger rises as the other descends affects the sound.

1. With your right-hand fingers on CDEFG, alternate D and E with fingers 2 and 3.
   - Note the pressure it takes for your finger to lower and hold each key.
   - Be careful to transfer this correct pressure from one note to the other in order to stay on pitch.
2. Practice connecting the two notes or detaching them slightly.
   - Note the difference in sound and feel when you play two notes in the middle as compared with two notes in the uppermost part of the keyboard.
3. With your left-hand fingers on CDEFG, repeat the previous exercise, alternating F and E with fingers 2 and 3.
   - Compare the feel and sound of notes in the middle with those in the lowermost parts of the keyboard.
4. When this exercise becomes easy, extend it to repetitions on other fingers, first on the right hand (example 3.5) and then on the left (example 3.6).

EXAMPLE 3.5

EXAMPLE 3.6

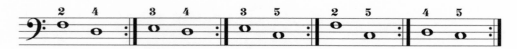

Lesson Four: Including a Raised Key

Sharps and flats are more difficult to control, since the keys are higher, shorter, and farther away from you. In order to position your fingertip securely on the raised key, you may lift and then lower your wrist ever so slightly.

1. Place your right-hand fingers comfortably close to the front ends of keys DEF♯GA.
2. Play E with finger 2 (example 3.7).

EXAMPLE 3.7

3. Raise finger 3 to play F♯ in a curved position, lifting your wrist very slightly if needed.
4. Gently lower your wrist to play E with finger 2 again.
5. Repeat E and F♯ slowly back and forth, using an easy, semidetached touch.
   - For quick repetitions, hold your wrist sufficiently high so that fingers 2 and 3 can move more freely.
   - Finger 2 is more curved than finger 3.
6. Repeat in reverse direction with your left hand, with finger 2 playing G and finger 3 playing F♯ (example 3.8).

EXAMPLE 3.8

Lesson Five: Bach's Cantabile Touch

The cantabile technique that I learned in Europe affected me deeply as an artist and teacher. Later, I found it corresponded with Johann Nicolaus Forkel's description of Johann Sebastian Bach's touch.

Forkel describes Bach's touch in his book *Über Johann Sebastian Bachs Leben, Kunst und Kunstwerke* (*On Johann Sebastian Bach's Life, Genius, and Works,* first published in Leipzig in 1802). He based his description partly on information he gleaned from Bach's son Emanuel. Since he describes the touch you will learn in subsequent lessons, Forkel's important quotations are included for your study.

> According to Sebastian Bach's manner of placing the hand on the keys, the five fingers are bent so that their tips form a straight line and . . . fit the keys, which lie in a plane surface under them. . . . [Thus] no single finger has to be drawn nearer when it is wanted, but each one is poised over the key that it may have to press down. What follows from this manner of holding the hand is:
>
> (1) That no finger must fall upon its key, or (as also often happens) be thrown on it, but only needs to be placed upon it with a certain consciousness of the internal power and command over the motion.
>
> (2) The impulse thus given to the keys, or the amount of pressure, must be maintained in equal strength, and in such a manner that the finger is not raised perpendicularly from the key, but glides off the front part of the key by gradually drawing the fingertip towards the palm of the hand.
>
> (3) In making the transition from one key to another, this gliding off causes the amount of force or pressure with which the first tone has been maintained to be transferred with the greatest rapidity to the next finger so that the two tones are neither disconnected from each other nor blended together. . . .
>
> Then the touch is, as C. Ph. Emanuel Bach says, neither too long nor too short, but just what it ought to be.
>
> There are various advantages for such a hand position and such a touch, not only on the clavichord, but also on the pianoforte and the organ. . . .
>
> (1) Holding the fingers bent makes all their motions easy. There need be none of the scrambling, thumping, and stumbling which is so common in persons who play with their fingers stretched out, or not sufficiently bent.
>
> (2) The drawing in of the fingertips and consequently the rapid communication of the force of one finger to the following produces the highest degree of clarity in the expression of the single tones. Thus every passage played in this way sounds brilliant, rolling, and round, as if each tone were a pearl. . . .

(3) By gliding the fingertip upon the key with an equal pressure, the string is given sufficient time in which to vibrate; thereby the tone is not only improved, but also prolonged, and we are enabled to play in a singing style and with proper connection.

In eighteenth-century Europe, instrumentalists were obliged to imitate the human voice. To encourage singing tones on the clavichord, this described way of playing will be referred to as the "cantabile" touch.

Lesson Six: Producing a Cantabile (Singing) Sound

In earlier lessons you pressed a key down and simply held it there. Now you are going to learn a better way to sustain the sound. By pressing and pulling forward on the key with your curled fingertip, you can hold the tangent evenly on the strings for a longer time. Plan to master this cantabile touch from the outset so you can create singing tones that are beautiful and controlled.

The size of your hand and fingers makes a difference in how the following exercises will be played. If you have large hands, your fleshy fingertips will hold down the keys more easily, and therefore the motion will be less. If you have slender fingers, motions will be quite visible at first, but this will lessen as you become accustomed to the cantabile touch.

1. Place your right-hand fingertips on CDEFG (or any successive naturals). Your nonplaying fingers should remain passive, lightly touching the surfaces of the keys (figure 3.1).

2. Press D and pull forward on the key with the fleshy part of your fingertip. Hook your finger as you caress or slightly claw the key.
   - As you glide your finger over the key, keep the pressure equal.

3. Release the key by continuing the motion of your fingertip inward and upward.

FIGURE 3.1

   - Your finger easily circles back to its resting position on the surface of the key.
   - Listen to the entire sound and the silence that follows.

4. With your left-hand fingertips on CDEFG, press and pull on F with your index finger, continuing the inward motion until after the key is released.

5. Repeat this exercise with finger 3 on E, first with the right hand and then with the left.

6. As you practice, the motions will become less perceptible.

Patience and focus are important in learning to produce a singing tone. Eventually and unexpectedly, your own sound will bloom.

Lesson Seven: Cantabile with Fingers 4 and 5

Babies grasp with all five fingers. Adults tend to use mainly the second and third fingers and the thumb. The clavichord, however, requires that all your fingers be active and independent.

The cantabile "grasping" touch is particularly helpful in strengthening fingers 4 and 5. These fingers tend to be weak and dependent on each other. To compensate, players often add the force of a tense, rigid wrist and thumb plus the useless motions of adjacent, nonplaying fingers.

Once you have begun to isolate your fourth and fifth fingers in a comfortable way, each will be able to develop its own strength. The following exercise will strengthen these two fingers and foster their independence so they can begin to produce cantabile tones.

1. Place the fingers of one hand lightly on four successive natural keys. (Allow your thumb to be free.)
2. To apply a cantabile touch, slowly press and pull forward on a key with your fourth finger, repeating several times.
    *   Be aware of the feel of your finger as it slides along the key.
    *   Note your finger's relationship to the tangent and the relationship of the key to the strings.
3. Rest, and then do the same with your fifth finger.
4. Repeat with your other hand.
    *   Each finger should begin its motion from the strong center point of its fleshy tip.
    *   To find and maintain this strong point, your mobile, relaxed wrist may need to tilt outward. Your forearm may move slightly outward as well.
    *   To isolate your fourth or fifth finger, try to keep your nonplaying fingers inactive.
    *   Listen to and accept the sound you make, even if it is faint.
    *   In time, as your fourth and fifth fingers become stronger, the tones they produce will grow and begin to sing.

Lesson Eight: Cantabile with the Thumb

Your thumb must be flexible and mobile to produce a cantabile sound. It needs special attention because it strokes the key sideways. With this in mind, several preliminary exercises are included.

Exercise 1: For a Relaxed Thumb

1. Rest one hand, palm up, in your lap.
2. Gently grasp the first joint of your thumb with your other hand.
3. Loosely rotate the entire thumb in a circle from its base, first clockwise and then counterclockwise.
   - François Couperin advised loosening inflexible fingers by pulling, or having them pulled, in all directions.

Exercise 2: For a Flexible Thumb

1. Place your right hand in playing position on a flat surface.
2. Practice sliding the first joint of your thumb back and forth towards and under the arch of your hand (figure 3.2).

FIGURE 3.2

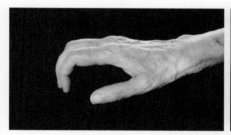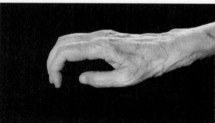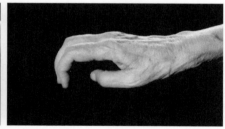

- Begin with a slight motion and gradually extend it until this joint is at right angles with your index finger.
- Keep the other joints of your thumb relaxed yet responsive.

Main Practice:
Producing a Cantabile Sound with Your Thumb

1. Place the five fingers of your right hand on CDEFG.
   - The left side of your fleshy thumbtip touches C (figure 3.3).
2. Press and hold down C, pulling your thumbtip sideways on the key toward your arched hand to produce a cantabile tone.
   - This sideways motion helps keep the pressure constant, making it easier to sustain a tone and stay on pitch.
   - Although this motion centers on the tip and first joint of the thumb, allow for a gentle reaction of the entire thumb, stemming from its base.

FIGURE 3.3

3. Release your thumb from C by following through with your thumbtip's motion as though you were flicking a piece of lint from a key.
   - Your relaxed thumb will bounce back to its initial position naturally.
4. Repeat with your left hand on CDEFG an octave below middle C. To play G, pull your thumbtip sideways toward the left.

With practice, your thumbs will become more mobile and nimble and capable of producing nuanced cantabile sounds.

Lesson Nine: Cantabile on Two Successive Notes

When playing two notes in sequence, transfer the pressure evenly from one finger to the other as if you were walking on two fingertips.

Exercise 1

With your fingers on CDEFG, apply the cantabile touch to fingers 2 and 3 of the right hand, slowly alternating D and E (figure 3.4).

- Press and pull one key at a time, emphasizing the independence of the two fingers.
- One fingertip pulls toward you while the other circles out to begin the next tone.
- Rather than overlap notes, release each finger toward your palm as you begin the next.
- Stay near the key ends and press evenly to keep on pitch.

FIGURE 3.4

Exercise 2

With the cantabile touch, play E and F with fingers 3 and 4 and then F and G with fingers 4 and 5.

- Allow for weak tones on fingers 4 and 5 rather than tensing up your wrist.
- Note how fingers 4 and 5 tend to cling together. Separating them without tension requires the utmost care.
- To achieve a clear tone on these fingers, each tip must be centered on its key.

Exercise 3

Practice carefully the following patterns for fingers 2, 3, 4, and 5 (example 3.9).

- Relax within each rest.

EXAMPLE 3.9

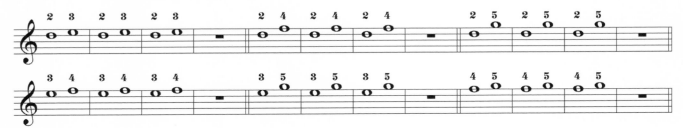

Exercise 4

1. Alternate C and D with your thumb and index finger. Press and pull your thumbtip sideways, using the cantabile touch.
   - The first thumb joint bends toward the index finger and may continue under it.
   - As the thumb circles back, finger 2 has room to play D as it pulls toward you.
2. Practice the following thumb patterns, relaxing within the rests (example 3.10).

EXAMPLE 3.10

Repeat all the exercises in this lesson with the left hand in reverse direction (example 3.11).

• Release each pattern of repeated notes and rest before you play the next.

EXAMPLE 3.11

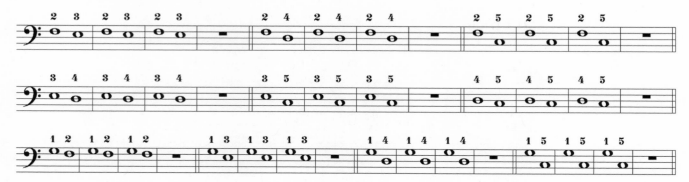

Lesson Ten: Playing Five Cantabile Tones in a Row

Rather than conceiving of five notes in a row as a unit, it is important to transfer your attention (and finger pressure) from one note to the next (figure 3.5).

1. With your right-hand fingertips on CDEFG, play five notes in sequence, ascending and descending. Listen to each sound while staying at ease (example 3.12).

EXAMPLE 3.12

2. Using the cantabile touch, slowly push down and pull inward with one finger, circling back as the next finger begins its motion. Your thumb will be moving sideways (figure 3.5).

FIGURE 3.5

- Let each fleshy fingertip find its strongest and most centered position on the key.
- For fingers 4 and 5 you may move your wrist slightly outward as you go up, returning to normal position as you return.
- As the notes ascend, relax your thumb, allowing it to move under your index finger. Particularly with a small hand, this may help you center fingers 4 and 5.
- As the notes descend, the thumb gradually returns to its normal position.

3. Repeat with the left hand in reverse motion (example 3.13).

EXAMPLE 3.13

Lesson Eleven: Timing

Playing with precise timing is not simple on the clavichord since there is no consistent pressure point at which the sound begins. This is particularly true for clavichords requiring significant differences in pressure from treble to bass.

Thus, from the beginning, it is important to learn to play in exact time. This involves controlling the tangent's contact with the strings. Your fingers and ears can become aware of making this happen for both sequential and simultaneous sounds. Acquiring such a skill will later enable you to explore the very subtle nuances in timing so essential for fine playing.

Exercise 1: Precision in Timing, Two Notes in Sequence

When playing notes in sequence, listen for precision in timing (example 3.14).

EXAMPLE 3.14

1. Go slowly and relax into the dotted notes, always maintaining the correct timing and pitch.
    - Focus on each sound as you play it, noting the finger weight required.
    - Isolate as much as possible the motion of each finger as it plays.
    - Give special attention to the fourth and fifth fingers, which are more difficult to control.
2. Repeat each pair of notes at least twice.

Exercise 2: Simultaneous Notes, One to a Hand

1. Play a sixth with your two index fingers.
    - Make sure they sound precisely at the same time.
    - Listen to the tones until they die away.
2. Play a sixth with your two middle fingers.
3. Play octaves with your two fourth fingers and then your fifth fingers, making sure the motion is made by the fingers alone and that the two notes sound precisely together.

Exercise 3: A Series of Successive Sixths

1. Play five sixths in a row, one note to a hand (example 3.15).

EXAMPLE 3.15

- Listen for the exact point both tangents come in contact with the strings.
- Go slowly, consciously sustaining the sounds of each interval.
- Release each interval and wait before you play the next.
- Keep your arms, wrists, and nonplaying fingers at ease.

Lesson Twelve:
Timing for Five-Finger Patterns, Both Hands

1. Play each hand separately until the pattern becomes easy (example 3.16).

EXAMPLE 3.16

- Center each fingertip and curl it slightly toward you while your nonplay-ing fingers remain relaxed.

2. Play both hands together, timing each pair of notes precisely.
   - Note how the timing of the thumb differs from the other fingers.
3. With your fingers over D, E, and F♯, play the same exercises with a sharp-ened F (example 3.17).

EXAMPLE 3.17

- Stretch out your third finger ever so slightly so that it can pull forward with a cantabile touch.
- A flexible wrist and arm will help you find the right position.
- Be sure each fingertip is centered so that your timing can be precise.
4. Finally, feel free to make up your own patterns until you can apply a sense of timing to simple pieces.

CHAPTER FOUR

Clavichord Lessons, Series II

WHEN YOU CAN play in time and in tune and begin to produce singing tones, other clavichord skills will open up for you. Gradually you will learn to make use of the subtle, expressive effects that are so natural to the clavichord.

Lesson One: Degrees of Softness

Of all keyboard instruments, the clavichord is the most capable of delicate, dynamic shading down to the softest pianissimo. These fine shadings are heard best by the player and a few listeners positioned near the clavichord's soundboard.

Shading on a clavichord involves many variables. Each key has its own shading possibilities. Likewise, each clavichord has its own range of dynamics. The breadth and subtleties of this range are interdependent on both your hands and your technique.

Variables include the soundboard's resonance, the depth of each key dip, the key's resistance to pressure, and the tautness or resilience of each set of strings from treble to bass.

With practice, you can take advantage of the dynamic spectrum of your clavichord. Eventually you will learn to adapt to various clavichords and their special needs. Basically, however, there is a special technique for achieving softer tones on the clavichord.

Exercise 1:
Producing a Decrescendo by Repeatedly Playing a Single Key

- For a full sound, start playing from the key level. Listen to how the tone fades by itself. This will affect the way you play the following tone.
- For a slightly softer sound, first lower the key a minute fraction of an inch so the tangent is closer to the strings. Then start at this level to produce, and hold, a tone.
- For still softer sounds, lower the key further by degrees before playing. It is like an elevator stopping at different floors.

The lower you begin and the more gently your finger strokes the key, the softer the sound will be until you hear no sound at all (figure 4.1).

FIGURE 4.1.

Exercise 2: Playing a Decrescendo on a Single Key at Various Points in the Treble and Bass

- Note the difference in the width of the key dip, the length of sound, and the range of shading you can achieve.

Eventually you will learn to adapt to various clavichords and their special characteristics. On fine clavichords of the fifteenth and sixteenth centuries, shades of dynamic possibilities are subtle, like the various tints of a miniature painting. You can use these shades very effectively to contour one voice and relate it to other voices. In contrast, large clavichords of the late eighteenth century offer a very wide dynamic range that allows you to extend crescendos and diminuendos for several measures, creating a new sense of drama.

It takes ability, curiosity, and patience to build a clavichord that shades well. Characteristics to consider include how the tone blooms, the amount of listing (dampening cloth), the balance of each key lever, the slant of the top of a tangent, and the way it strikes the strings.

A clavichord maker in my area specializes in large clavichords based on the work of Pehr Lindholm, an eighteenth-century Swedish builder. Already in the 1960s I had admired and performed on Lindholm clavichords in Europe, and eventually I brought a Lindholm home. Recently I showed the local maker that although he had achieved the louder colors of Lindholms, the very facile action of his keys made it difficult to shade softer tones. "Just push the keys harder," he said. Then he decided to explore. Usually he balanced a key lever by weighting it with lead at the far end (the easy way). Now he carefully cut out a little wood from under the playing end of the key lever, treating each lever on its own. When the clavichord was finished, we found it could be shaded effortlessly down to an exquisite pianissimo!

Lesson Two: Degrees of Loudness

There is an illusion of loudness on the clavichord that comes from starting at a very soft level and in the following notes suddenly or gradually increasing the sound. Emanuel Bach's sudden shifts from pianissimo to fortissimo, for example, can be shockingly dramatic (example 4.1).

EXAMPLE 4.1   The ending of Emanuel Bach's *Probestücke* no. 5 (1753), *Adagio assai mesto e sostenuto*

Other ways of affecting the loudness of a sound are as follows. (The latter two are for when you are more advanced.)

- Play as closely as you can to the edge of the key to make the sound full and clear.
- Vary the speed and force with which your hooked finger plays the key, but be careful not to drive the tone above pitch.
- Choose special fluctuations in pitch that can strengthen and lengthen a tone. The *portato* allows for one pitch fluctuation. The *Bebung* (or vibrato) customarily consists of four or more.
- Apply arm weight to make the tone louder. This depends, however, on the clavichord and on your ability to control the tangent. As a beginner it is important to focus on developing your finger independence while keeping your arm relaxed.

Exercise 1:
Playing a Crescendo with One Finger on a Single Note

- For a very soft sound, lower the key as far as possible before playing so the tangent will be very close to the strings. Then play from the edge of the key.

- To make each subsequent sound a little louder, lower the key slightly less each time. The tangent will have progressively more and more space in which to build momentum for striking the strings.

- For a full tone, play from key level.

- For an even louder sound, strengthen the force of your hooked finger and quicken the speed. Remember to keep the pitch constant.

Lesson Three:
Crescendo and Diminuendo on Five Notes

After you have learned to play a crescendo and a diminuendo separately, you will be ready to combine them.

1. Slowly make a crescendo on five ascending notes in the right hand (say, CDEFG) using the technique you have learned. Begin very softly below key level and gradually get louder until, at key level, you quickly grasp the key.

2. Then make a decrescendo (diminuendo), gradually getting softer as you descend (example 4.2).

EXAMPLE 4.2

- Your thumb and wrist stay flexible so that each finger can be centered on its own key for a singing tone.
- In order to keep your fourth and fifth fingers in strong positions, you may flex your wrist outward as you ascend and return it to a normal position as you descend.
- Take the time to listen very carefully to each note and see how smoothly you can make the gradual shift in dynamics while staying on pitch.

3. Repeat the process in the left hand on CDEFG. Notice the difference in pressure required in the bass (example 4.3).

EXAMPLE 4.3

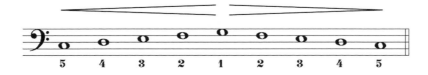

4. Experiment slowly with crescendos and diminuendos on other patterns, always aiming for smooth dynamic lines.

Lesson Four: Contrast in Dynamics, Two Hands

Eventually you will want to shade each voice separately and show how it relates to other voices. At this point, you may try the following simple exercises, keeping the wrist relaxed:

Exercise 1:
Dynamic Contrast between Two Simultaneous Tones

1. Choose two notes for your middle fingers to play (such as G above and C below middle C).
2. Play both notes together, making G loud with the right hand and C soft with the left by lowering the key before playing. Hold and listen.
3. Reverse, with G soft in the right hand and C loud in the left. Hold and listen as the sounds fade away.

Exercise 2: Dynamic Contrast between Two Notes in a Row Using a Semi-detached Touch

1. In the right hand play A and B at full volume with fingers 2 and 3 while playing C and D softer in the left hand with fingers 3 and 2.
2. Now play C and D in the left hand at full volume while playing A and B softer in the right.
3. Be sure to play notes of both hands exactly together.

Exercise 3: Experiment with Other Fingers and Other Keys

Lesson Five:
Articulation on Single Notes with One Finger

As with shading, articulation need not be limited to several possibilities. Legato and staccato can be extended to many subtle degrees of tonal connection and separation. The cantabile touch will give you access to this wider range of articulation.

1. With your right or left index finger, press and pull on any key you wish (figure 4.2).

FIGURE 4.2

- Take time to catch and hold the key in order to sustain the sound.
- Release the key by continuing to curl your finger toward the palm of your hand.

2. Now pull, hold, and release your finger, but shorten the time you hold the note to allow a space of silence before playing the next note.
   - At first, make the space of silence very small.
   - Gradually quicken your finger motion to lessen the length of sound and increase the length of silence.
   - Begin flicking your finger toward your palm so that the silence lasts longer than the sound.
   - Flick the key ever more quickly so that the silence lasts ever longer.
   - End with a crisp staccato.
3. Repeat the exercise on various notes from bass to treble to see how articulation can differ.
4. Now try the same exercise with other fingers, but do not force them.
   - With the fourth and fifth fingers, play from the strong point on their tips, keeping a flexible wrist.
   - With the thumb moving sideways, pull, hold, and release the key.

Gradually your motions should become more natural and less and less extreme.

On fretted clavichords, descending notes cannot be completely connected when two or more tangents strike the same set of strings. (There is an art to making the separations so minuscule that the tones seem almost joined.) On unfretted clavichords, all sounds can be sustained, and the range of detachment and connection can be very wide. Gradually take advantage of what your clavichord can do.

Lesson Six: Articulation on Two Notes

Exercise 1: For Index and Third Fingers

1. With your right-hand fingers over CDEFG, play D and E in succession with fingers 2 and 3.
   - Be aware of how the keys, tangents, and strings respond.
2. Repeat the same two notes, gradually going from an over-legato to a very quick staccato. The possible variations become greater as you learn to apply this technique (figure 4.3).
   - "Walk" in place with padded fingertips on D and E so that for a moment both notes sound at the same time. (Overlap the motions of finger 2 and finger 3 as they pull forward on the keys.)
   - Lessen the overlapping of your two fingers as you play.
   - Release finger 2 exactly as the tip of finger 3 begins to play.
   - Leave a tiny space between the sounds of two notes, still continuing to suggest a singing line.
   - For greater degrees of staccato, let this space gradually grow. The sound becomes ever more detached as though skipping.
   - For a sharp staccato, flick the finger abruptly as if the key were very hot.

FIGURE 4.3

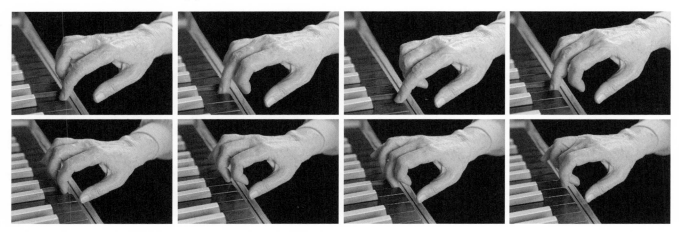

3. Reverse the above procedure, progressing from extreme staccato to an overlapping of tones.
4. Play the entire exercise with the left hand with fingers 2 and 3 on F and E.

Exercise 2: Articulation for Other Pairs of Fingers

1. Now practice exercises for the right hand as shown in example 4.4. For each pair, proceed from over-legato to a very quick staccato and then back to an over-legato. Be careful to keep the wrist and thumb relaxed.

EXAMPLE 4.4

2. Do the same with the left hand, as shown in example 4.5.

EXAMPLE 4.5

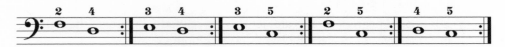

3. Now play two-note patterns for the thumb and another finger as shown in example 4.6. Move the thumb sideways while pulling the other finger forward, keeping the wrist relaxed.

EXAMPLE 4.6

Lesson Seven: Leaping with One Finger

When you leap from one note to another, move from your wrist and elbow, relaxing your hand. Be aware of how your finger leaves one key and lands lightly on the surface of the next.

Exercise 1: Leaping Silently

1. With the second or third fingertip of your right or left hand, lightly touch any key, such as middle C (figure 4.4).
2. As you leap up (or down) an interval of two octaves, let your wrist and hand float like a dancer, fingertips suspended, pointing toward the keyboard.

FIGURE 4.4

3. Land on the next note lightly (like a butterfly), gently touching the key without making a sound.
4. Leap back and forth easily between the two octaves, again without any sound.
5. With your eyes closed, leap back and forth even more slowly.
6. Choose other fingers and other intervals.

Exercise 2: Leaping with Sound

Now try the same leaping exercise, but this time add sounds.

1. Play middle C with the third finger of your right hand. Be careful to remain on pitch as you leave the key.
2. Leap two octaves higher, your hand and wrist floating and your fingers hovering over the keys.
3. Land soundlessly with your third finger on the surface of the second key.
4. Immediately press and pull forward on the key to make a tone.
5. Listen to the tone sing.
6. Repeat with your left hand, leaping downward. Notice any difference in pressure required to lower the key.

Exercise 3: Experiment with Other Fingers and Other Distances between the Notes

Lesson Eight: Playing Intervals with One Hand

To play an interval, press and pull and then hold both keys evenly, as though slightly grasping them. This will approximate the cantabile touch and give you a more sustained control.

Exercise 1: Play and Repeat a Third with Fingers 2 and 4

1. Place your five fingers on CDEFG an octave above middle C.
2. Pull in gently and soundlessly on the surface of D and F with fingers 2 and 4 while keeping the other fingers still.
3. Now press and pull and hold D and F with your fingers, producing sounds.

    *   Be sure tones of the interval are played simultaneously unless you purposely want to play one note after the other.
    *   Hold the keys steadily to keep the tangent pressure and the sound constant.
    *   Nonplaying fingers should remain passive, and your wrist should remain relaxed.

Exercise 2: Intervals Involving the Thumb

Now try playing intervals of a fifth, sixth, and finally an octave that involve the thumb (examples 4.7 and 4.8).

*   At key level, hook your thumb and finger and "grasp" the keys by descending and pulling inward toward the palm of your hand.
*   Hold the pressure constant while relaxing your wrist and arm quickly.
*   For a louder interval, grasp more strongly.
*   Larger hands require less effort.

EXAMPLE 4.7

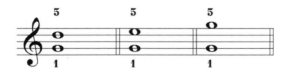

EXAMPLE 4.8

Exercise 3: Contrast between Legato and Staccato for One Interval

This exercise is to awaken you to treating multiple notes in one hand individually.

1. Touch, for example, a fifth with fingers 1 and 5.
2. Play both notes together as you have been.
3. Now hold one key while quickly releasing the other.
    *   Both fingers pull inward toward the palm of the hand, but one finger immediately follows through with its motion.
    *   For the held note, be sure to keep the pressure steady until the key is finally released.
4. Try different intervals in this way.

Exercise 4: Grasping Paper with Your Fingers

Finally, with one hand, take hold of the corner of a newspaper page. Gradually wad it up with just your fingertips until it forms a little ball. Keep the wrist and arm relaxed.

Lesson Nine: Passagework with a Flexible Thumb

Passagework on the clavichord requires special attention, since the smallest motion will have an effect. The natural inequality of your five fingers in strength and control is particularly evident on this instrument. Sometimes this inequality can be used to advantage, and sometimes it must be counteracted.

Using a constant legato on the clavichord for passagework can neutralize the music. For the most part, subtle variations in articulation and dynamics are more vivifying on this instrument. A slightly detached touch also makes a difference in the ease with which passagework can be played. It can even give the impression of a clean "legato" or make possible a wide variety of fingerings.

Only with the eighteenth century did new tunings encourage the use of twenty-four scales. In certain of these scales, such as that of B major, "modern" fingerings are natural. They require, however, a highly mobile thumb.

In scale passages in general, the thumb can easily go under the other fingers because of its shortness. In *School of Clavier Playing*, Türk remarks: "When one places (bends or pulls) the thumb . . . gradually under the longer fingers," it can "creep under unnoticeably."[1]

At this point, it is helpful to review the thumb exercises offered in Chapter 3. Then apply the following exercises for the thumb's use in scales.

Exercise 1: For a Flexible Thumb on the Scale of B Major

With fingers 2 and 3 touching C♯ and D♯, gently tap keys B and then E with your thumbtip, back and forth.

- Your entire nimble thumb, down to its base, should react naturally.
- Your wrist and forearm should stay loose and mobile.

Exercise 2: Six Notes of the B Major Scale,
Involving the Thumb

1. To go up the scale, place fingers 123 of your right hand over keys B, C♯, and D♯.

2. Play B with your thumb, pulling it sideways on the key, allowing it to keep moving toward the right in an easy way.
   - Proceed slowly, with a nonlegato cantabile touch and a slight motion of your entire arm in the direction the scale is going.

3. Your thumb arrives under finger 2 as this finger plays C♯.

4. Continue moving your thumb gradually to the right so that it is almost under finger 3 when it plays D♯.

5. Meanwhile, continue to shift your whole hand and arm slightly toward the right so that when the thumb plays E, it can pivot easily without overpressing the key.

6. Keep the thumb relatively in place as you play F♯ and G♯ with fingers 2 and 3.

7. On the return, fingers 2 and 3 move easily over the thumb as it pulls toward the right and then circles back gradually under D♯ and C♯ to play B again.

In the eighteenth century, "modern" scale fingering was not obligatory. As late as 1789, Türk gave multiple fingerings for such scales as C and G major. One of them, common in prior centuries, is included to awaken your fingers to "new" possibilities. Try it on C major, using a semidetached touch and staying close to the keys. Move the entire arm in the direction of the scale passage so that finger motion can be minimal.

Right hand: 12343434, 43212121

Left hand: 43212121, 12343434

As time goes on, you may wish to explore the semi-detached lines that give the impression of being "legato." Likewise, you may wish to train your fingers to play various early fingerings. Rather than being primitive or clumsy, these fingerings can help you play suitable music with finesse. Details on different fingerings are offered later, in Chapters 7 and 8.

CHAPTER FIVE

Preparing for Pieces

BEFORE YOU BEGIN to play short pieces of the eighteenth century, it is important to have a repertoire of basic ornaments. At that time, beginners on the clavichord were first taught to play ornaments without music. You too may begin with individual ornaments, learning to make them clean and even. This is not simple on the clavichord, since its touch is so flexible. It is this touch, however, that will eventually free you to express the most delicate ornamental details. Like variations in dynamics and articulation (and affected by them both), ornaments can become a very subtle aspect of your playing.

In general, rapid ornaments are easier to play on the harpsichord. Plucking a string with a plectrum is more precise than striking and pressing it with a tangent. In fact, practicing ornaments on the harpsichord can help you think of them distinctly, keeping in mind that the sound point on the clavichord will be inexact unless controlled.

To prepare for playing ornaments on the clavichord, I have included an exercise (example 5.1). Play it from key level, slowly and attentively, making sure you use a clavichord touch. Then try short groups a little faster as you are able. You may relax after the last note of each group.

EXAMPLE 5.1

After you can play example 5.1 with ease, you may extend it, but very slowly, to all five fingers in example 5.2. To play the notes equally requires the utmost attention on the clavichord.

EXAMPLE 5.2

1. Place your five right-hand fingers over GABCD (example 5.2).
2. Play the exercise slowly, keeping the wrist relaxed. Take time to rest whenever needed.
   - Make sure to position the thumb and fingers 4 and 5 correctly, paying special attention to their power and independence.
   - Rather than tense the fingers, keep them flexible and free.
3. Now play this exercise in the left hand with your fingers over CDEFG (example 5.3).

EXAMPLE 5.3

In 1720 J. S. Bach gave his young son Wilhelm Friedemann a little music book in which he included a table of ornaments. Five of them, in his handwriting, are pictured in figure 5.1. Before proceeding, examine them carefully.

FIGURE 5.1

The Trill

For eighteenth-century music, the most important ornament for a beginner is the trill. Since it is difficult, Emanuel Bach says it must be "practiced diligently from the start."[1] The eventual aim is to enhance a melody by finger strokes that are uniform, light, and rapid. Tendons must stay relaxed, or the trill will "grow ragged" or "bleat."[2]

In his *School of Clavier Playing* (1789), Daniel Gottlob Türk writes specifically about the clavichord.[3] He says, in essence, to first play the trill slowly with fingers 2 and 3. For beginners, the upper note tends to be weaker and faster than the lower. Only when the notes are equal in strength and speed (and stay on pitch) can the player begin to play the trill more rapidly.[4]

Listed here are the basic types of trills, according to Emanuel Bach and Türk:

1. A short trill is the most necessary and attractive of all trills, yet it is only effective when played very fast. At first, try it slowly to be sure of the proper touch. Then link it to the preceding note and see if you can make it crackle with great speed. Keep your fingers close to the keys except for the last upper note, which rebounds quickly from the key while the final lower note is held securely on pitch (example 5.4).[5]

EXAMPLE 5.4

2. For a long trill, the notes must be even.

EXAMPLE 5.5

The last upper note is snapped quickly. "After the stroke, the upper joint of the finger is sharply doubled and drawn off the key [toward the palm] as quickly as possible."[6] Thus the next finger, holding a specific pitch, "may play its tone distinctly" (example 5.5).[7]

3. A trill on a long note can be smoothed out with a suffix such as the mordent (as in J. S. Bach's example at the beginning of this lesson).[8] The suffix is played close to the keys as rapidly and easily as the trill itself.[9] This adds grace to the trill's ending and connects it to the next note. Example 5.6 shows a trill with an added mordent as a suffix.

EXAMPLE 5.6

4. Finally, Türk offers the following suggestions, to be applied when you are quite advanced:

   - Learn to play the trill with different degrees of intensity, increasing and decreasing the volume without varying the speed.

   - In the bass, play trills more slowly, since they are less easily perceived.

   - A very rapid trill is appropriate only for a small, intimate setting. In a large room or a hall it becomes ineffective, particularly if the listener is far away.

   - The loudness and softness of your trills depend on the music's character and above all on each musical thought you wish to express.

The Mordent

The mordent is pointed, precise, and lively.[10] A short, fast mordent adds brilliance to ascending stepwise notes and leaps. Of all embellishments, the mordent is used most frequently in the bass. By practicing this ornament as well as trills on the clavichord, you will learn to control your instrument when playing quickly and distinctly.

1. For a short mordent, play G and F♯ on fingers 323 in the right hand and fingers 232 in the left (example 5.7).

EXAMPLE 5.7

- With finger 3 of your right hand, play G and stay close to the key while you quickly play F♯ by pulling your index finger toward you and upward in a curl.
- Repeat G, holding the pressure constant to the end.
- Move your fingers only as quickly and nimbly as you are able.
- Keep the sounds equal and on pitch by controlling each finger motion.

2. For a long mordent, play the notes in example 5.8.

EXAMPLE 5.8

- Keep your two fingers close to the keys and your wrist loose.
- Quickly curl your second finger upward on its last play.
- Do not force the final note, but hold the pressure steady.

According to Emanuel Bach, "when mordents serve to fill out a long note, a small fraction of the original length remains free of decoration."[11]

The Turn

The turn is usually played rapidly on the beat. It is appropriate for connected or detached tones and different tempi, as seen in example 5.9. The first three notes are in quick sequence, and the last note is held except in the Presto.

EXAMPLE 5.9

1. Practice the turn with 4323 in the right hand and 2343 in the left.
   - The first finger is played with a snap, pulling it forward and upward.
   - The second finger stays close to the key so that it is ready to play again.
   - The third finger on F♯ is very slightly extended but quickly pulled forward and up in a snap.
2. Keep the final tone on pitch by catching the key and holding it like a hook, except when playing presto.

The Appoggiatura

The appoggiatura is particularly beautiful on the clavichord because this instrument is capable of minute variations in shading. The pronounced dissonance on the upper (or lower) auxiliary note resolves smoothly to a consonance that can be as soft as a whisper. According to Emanuel Bach, "appoggiaturas enhance harmony as well as melody" by "modifying chords which would be too simple without them." "Some appoggiaturas vary in length," he says, while "others are always rapid."[12]

An "invariable appoggiatura" lasts only a brief time, irrespective of the length of the note that follows. It can be as short as a sixty-fourth note in slow tempo, a thirty-second note in moderate tempo, or a sixteenth note in very fast tempo. This ornament is easier to play rapidly because each note occurs only once (example 5.10).

EXAMPLE 5.10

The long "variable appoggiatura" offers more opportunity for nuanced expression. In earlier times it was simply written as an eighth note, allowing the player flexibility in timing. Eighteenth-century composers wrote out appoggiaturas in full or indicated them by tiny notes that varied in length from a half note to a thirty-second note (example 5.11).

EXAMPLE 5.11

The time of this note is stolen from the chord tone that follows, taking up to half or even more of the latter's value. It may be extended even further for voice leading or for a special emotional affect.

Clearly, all you have learned about dynamic shading is relevant here. Your ability to lower a key to different levels while playing an appoggiatura offers you a variety of soft, often spontaneous tonal options. This, combined with subtleties in timing and articulation, can help you create a wide range of moods ranging from playful shyness to tragic sighing.

The *Bebung*

No word about clavichord ornaments would be complete without mentioning the famous *Bebung.* Here you apply the clavichord's unique capability for oscillating the pitch of a note by purposely wavering the tangent's pressure against the strings. This ornament is excellent for sustaining long notes and intensifying moments of high emotion (example 5.12).

EXAMPLE 5.12

To produce a *Bebung,* Gottlob Türk says, "the finger is allowed to remain on the key for as long as is required by the duration of the given note and tries to reinforce the tone with a repeated and gentle pressure. . . . After each pressure there is a lessening, but . . . the finger should not be completely lifted off the key."[13]

Emanuel Bach adds: "A long *affettuoso* tone is performed with a *Bebung.* The finger that depresses and holds the key is gently rocked. . . . The best effect is achieved when the finger withholds its vibrato until half the value of the note has passed."[14]

According to the English writer Charles Burney, Emanuel Bach was a master of the *Bebung.* "In the pathetic and slow movements, whenever he had a long note to express, he absolutely contrived to produce, from his instrument, a cry of sorrow and complaint such as can only be effected upon the clavichord; and perhaps by himself."[15]

Examples of Emanuel Bach's *Bebung* are found in the *Largo maestoso* from his *Probestücke,* published in 1753 (example 5.13). Note the five dots under each slur rather than the customary four. For exceptionally long notes, Bach used as many as twelve.

EXAMPLE 5.13

To create a *Bebung:*

1. With your hand in playing position, lower and hold a key with your third finger so the tangent presses against the strings.
2. Vary the pressure by pulsating your finger, going farther down on the key (pulling forward slightly) and then up again without releasing the tangent from the strings. This causes the pitch to fluctuate.
3. Return to the original pressure (and pitch) and hold.
   - Listen to the way the tone begins, blooms as it trembles, and finally fades away.
   - If you push the key down too aggressively, you can produce a nasty twang.
   - To avoid tension, you may gradually raise your limber wrist very slightly while you play.

The degree, quality, and speed of the *Bebung* depend on your clavichord, its stringing, your personal technique, and the music you have chosen.

Tragen der Töne (*Portato*)

Again, the clavichord is the only keyboard instrument on which the *Tragen der Töne* can be made. By holding down a key and slowly swaying it vertically once, you can reinforce a tone so that it is sustained or connected to the next note. In the time of Emanuel Bach, the *Tragen der Töne* was indicated as shown in example 5.14.

EXAMPLE 5.14

1. Play the *Tragen der Töne* on one note, first with the third finger of your right hand and then with your left.

    • Raise the tangent to normal pressure against the strings.

    • Without releasing it, push the tangent a little higher against the strings to elevate the pitch.

    • Return the tangent to its original pressure and hold it there.

2. When you are able to manipulate the *Tragen der Töne* correctly, you can use it to prolong or emphasize certain notes and intensify emotion in the music you are playing.

Ornaments in General

In earlier times clavichordists customarily added their own ornaments. Emanuel Bach, however, regarded an excess of all embellishments as "spices [that] may ruin the best dish or gewgaws, which may deface the most perfect building."[16] At the same time he believed, "Many passages allow for more than one kind of embellishment. In such cases, the art of variation may be used to advantage: introduce first a caressing ornament, then a brilliant one; or . . . play the notes exactly as written . . . but always further the true affect."[17]

According to Emanuel, added ornaments in general should reflect the character of the music played. They can call attention to an important note and modify the tone for each affect.

The eighteenth-century Germanic ornaments that Emanuel Bach and Türk used have been emphasized in this chapter. Various ways of embellishing used in earlier centuries are also available to you today. As you extend your repertoire, it will be important to study those sources appropriate for the music you wish to play.

Pieces in the next chapter contain examples of the ornaments described above. First, practice these ornaments alone until they feel comfortable. Then play the music without ornaments. Finally, include the ornaments as an essential part of the musical line.

Ornaments are meant to reflect the character of your music. In fact, each ornament should have a special meaning. As you become acquainted with various embellishments, they will add to the expressiveness of your playing.

CHAPTER SIX

Eleven Easy Pieces

THE FOLLOWING MINIATURE pieces are included for your enjoyment as you advance from exercises to music. In order to apply and perfect what you have learned, proceed slowly and attentively.

1. Begin by playing a single voice, one phrase at a time, omitting the ornaments. Aim for clear, singing sounds that stay on pitch.
2. For pieces of two parts, play one voice and sing the other. Then play both parts, noting how they combine.
3. Later, you may add ornaments, first playing them alone and then listening to how they can enhance the music.
4. Feel free from the first to respond to the music's mood.

Daniel Gottlob Türk (1750–1813)

You already know of Türk as a clavichord master and follower of Emanuel Bach. His delightful, much appreciated *Little Pieces for Future Clavichordists* (*Kleine Handstücke für angehende Klavierspieler*) appeared in two volumes in 1792.

EXAMPLE 6.1   Daniel Gottlob Türk, "Die beyden Siechen" (Two languishing ones)

EXAMPLE 6.2   Daniel Gottlob Türk, "Leise nur, wie Zephrs Hauch"
(Gentle, like Zephyr's breath)

EXAMPLE 6.3   Daniel Gottlob Türk, "Jugendlicher Frohsinn"
(Youthful joy) (*notes with points are detached*)

EXAMPLE 6.4   Daniel Gottlob Türk, "Die Zufriedenheit" (Contentment)

Andante tranquillamente

Johann Wilhelm Hässler (1747–1822)

Hässler studied with Johann Christian Kittel, a favored pupil of J. S. Bach in his last years, and later taught the clavichordist Türk. He knew Emanuel Bach and greatly admired his work. In midlife Hässler moved to Russia, where he succeeded as a performer and a composer of fantasias in the style of Emanuel Bach.

This menuetto comes from Hässler's *50 Pieces for Beginners* (*50 pièces à l'usage des commençants*), op. 38.

EXAMPLE 6.5   Johann Wilhelm Hässler, Menuetto, no. 1

Christian Petzold (1677–1733)

J. S. Bach gave a beautiful leather notebook to his young second wife, Anna Magdalena, in 1725. For more than fifteen years pieces were added, many in Anna Magdalena's handwriting. This minuet in G minor comes from a suite by Christian Petzold, court organist of Dresden. Since cultured people customarily took both music and dance lessons, minuets were particularly popular in Germany at that time.

EXAMPLE 6.6 (*facing*)   Christian Petzold, Menuet in G Minor, BWV anh. 115, *Little Notebook for Anna Magdalena Bach*

Wolfgang Mozart (1756–1791)

Leopold Mozart gave his gifted daughter, Nannerl, a notebook in 1759. On its blank pages were penned some of his son Wolfgang's first attempts at playing and composing.

EXAMPLE 6.7   Wolfgang Mozart, Menuet in C Major (c. 1762)

Francesco Pasquale Ricci (1732–1817)

Francesco Ricci, *maestro di cappella* of the cathedral in Como, Italy, composed one hundred delightful keyboard pieces for beginners. He published them in The Hague in 1779 and also helped publish the music of Josina van Boetzelaer, his favored pupil. Ricci's pieces circulated widely throughout Europe and in the United States.

EXAMPLE 6.8 Francesco Pasquale Ricci, Andantino, no. 20

EXAMPLE 6.9 Francesco Pasquale Ricci, Andante, no. 22

EXAMPLE 6.10 Francesco Pasquale Ricci, Spiritoso, no. 23 (*last low Fs omitted*)

Stop at the fermata or add
some notes if you wish.

EXAMPLE 6.11   Francesco Pasquale Ricci, Andante affinnaso, no. 37

CHAPTER SEVEN

Exploring the Past: Fifteenth through Seventeenth Centuries

THE CLAVICHORD HAS an amazingly rich heritage from the centuries before Johann Sebastian Bach. This chapter offers glimpses of that time, involving the instrument and its music, its patrons, composers, and performers. May they inspire you to explore on your own the wealth of early material so readily available today.[1]

Although the clavichord's origins remain a mystery, by the fifteenth century it was popular among the educated throughout Europe. Young students began music lessons on the clavichord, and both nobility and monastics were enthusiasts. Artworks show angels and monks playing portable clavichords. Examples are in Bernard Brauchli's *The Clavichord,* a book you may wish to read.

Burgundian Lands

Henri Arnaut de Zwolle (c. 1400–1466)

The clavichord shown in figure 7.1 was built according to a diagram and description from the c. 1440 manuscript by Henri Arnaut de Zwolle.[2] This astrologer, physician, and organist served Philip the Good, duke of Burgundy. His court attracted and brought fame to some of the finest artists and musicians of the fifteenth century.

The clavichord pictured is so light that it can be carried under one arm. Short keys cover a span of three octaves. Since it has at most ten pairs of strings of equal length, the instrument is heavily fretted, with up to five tangents touching the same set of strings.[3]

Compelling pieces for this early clavichord exist in fifteenth-century collections of keyboard music. Among them is the so-called *Buxheimer Orgelbuch* (c. 1460), unearthed from a German monastery over a century ago.[4] The title *Orgelbuch,* however, is a misnomer. Keyboard tablatures were rarely confined to a specific instrument. In fact, it is rare to find any music written expressly for the clavichord. Yet many keyboard works are suitable for this instrument.

The *Buxheimer Orgelbuch* contains keyboard versions of vocal music by famed Guillaume Dufay, who taught Charles the Bold, the next duke of Burgundy. It seems

FIGURE 7.1 Joan Benson with a clavichord after Arnaut de Zwolle, built by John Altstatt, California, 1973

his third wife owned a devotional book of illuminated miniatures that includes a man playing the clavichord as he kneels before the Lamb of God.

After Charles died in battle in 1477, his daughter Mary of Burgundy guarded her inherited lands by marrying Maximilian of the Habsburg Dynasty. Her artistic world included daily clavichord lessons from a Flemish master organist. Still young, she was fatally injured while falcon hunting with her husband.

Maximilian now controlled large portions of Burgundy, including Flanders (involving today's Belgium and Holland). Much later he became king of the Germans and Holy Roman emperor.

The Habsburg Dynasty

Maximilian I (1459–1519)

As an important ruler, Maximilian I enjoyed promoting his own glory through the arts. His inflated autobiography contains a woodcut depicting him as a young king surrounded by court musicians and their instruments, among them a clavichord.

Hans Buchner (1483–1538)

Maximilian I's eminent court composer-organist, Paul Hofhaimer (1459–1537), had a pupil, Hans Buchner, who apparently replaced him when he was away. Later Buchner served as cathedral organist in Constance, Germany. Typically, he would have played the clavichord as well. In his treatise *Fundamentum* (c. 1525), Buchner offers very early fingerings that differ widely from those in use today.[5]

Buchner believed that "if [the fingers] are in their places, they cause a marvelous grace and delight."[6] Although he hesitated to give set fingerings, he advised using only the three middle fingers for patterns of eighth notes, as found in example 7.1.[7]

Try playing these patterns. They suggest a slightly detached touch particularly suitable for the extensively fretted clavichords of his day. Rather than twisting or overlapping your middle fingers, shift your entire hand and arm horizontally in the direction the notes are moving. Keep your wrist flexible and your thumb, when inactive, lower than the short keys.

EXAMPLE 7.1 Hans Buchner, *Fundamentum* (c. 1525)

In his treatise Buchner included a fingered keyboard tablature on the hymn "Quem terra, pontus, aethera colunt, adorant" (Whom earth, sea, and sky honor and adore) (example 7.2).[8] This medieval hymn praising the Virgin Mary appears initially as a cantus firmus (fixed melody) in the bass. Example 7.2 ends with the initial note of the cantus firmus in the treble, accentuated by a mordent.

First, sing the chant melody found in the bass. Next, practice the upper part with the correct fingering until it seems easy. Then, combine singing and playing. Finally, play both parts together.

EXAMPLE 7.2   Hans Buchner, "Quem terra pontus"

A facsimile of the original tablature is shown in figure 7.2. Note how spaces take the place of bar lines. The fingers are numbered 1–4 from the index to the little finger. The less-used thumb is numbered 5.

FIGURE 7.2

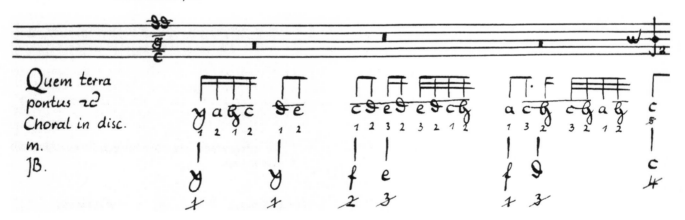

The celebrated Flemish composer Heinrich Isaac (1450–1517) became part of Maximilian's court in the last decades of their respective lives. Keyboard intabulations of vocal works by Isaac and other composers can sound exquisite when played on a fine, early clavichord.[9]

A keyboard version of Isaac's "Gracieuse plaisante" (Gracious pleasantry) may be found in the Codex of Bonifacius Amerbach (1495–1562).[10] The beginning is given in example 7.3. Note how the highly ornamented subject A(A)FED is repeated on an upper voice as D(D)BAG. Try playing this music with a constant legato and see how dull and clumsy it sounds. Then play it with a variety of detachments, acknowledging the main notes, and listen to it spring to life.

EXAMPLE 7.3   Heinrich Isaac, "Gracieuse plaisante" (Gracious pleasantry)

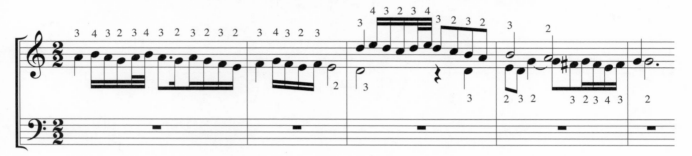

Philip the Fair (1478–1506)

The Habsburgs, in seeking to extend their power, used bold music for propaganda. Trumpets and drums accompanied their clamorous entrances into cities. By contrast, in their elegant personal lives they delighted in the soft, intimate tones of the clavichord.

In 1494 Maximilian I gave over his Burgundian lands to his teenage son, Philip the Fair. Philip traveled about with his Flemish *grande chapelle.* Included among its many singers, instrumentalists, and chaplains was the organ and clavichord master Henri Bredemers (1472–1522).[11]

Young Philip was the first Habsburg to travel to Spain, for the purpose of gaining territories through his wife, the "mad" Princess Juana of Castile. Bringing his Flemish *grande chapelle* with him, he asked Henri Bredemers to buy a clavichord, perhaps for daily private masses.[12]

Months after Philip was proclaimed ruler over Juana's lands, he died unexpectedly, possibly from poisoning. His sister Margaret of Austria became regent of the Habsburg Netherlands and guardian of Philip's children. Margaret wrote poetry and played several instruments. She encouraged painters such as Jan Vermeyen, who made a pen and ink drawing of a lady clavichord player.[13]

In Margaret's Flemish palace with its rich library, Master Bredemers gave the children daily clavichord lessons. The eldest child, Eleanor (later queen of France), became greatly admired in courts for her expressive clavichord playing.[14] Her sister Isabella (later queen of Denmark) asked Bredemers to buy a clavichord for her maid of honor. Their brother Charles also took daily clavichord lessons with Bredemers. At age eight, Charles played the clavichord during his protective country isolation from an outbreak of the plague.

Charles V (1500–1558)

In his teens, Charles took over the Habsburg Burgundian lands and became king of Castile and Aragon. His first entry into Valladolid, Spain, involved a triumphant royal procession, with trumpets and drums placed on the backs of horses. Charles's twelve Flemish trumpeters likely combined with twelve Castilian court trumpeters.[15] The arrival of the powerful Hapsburg dynasty would lead to Spain's Golden Era.

Charles retained Bredemers as organist in his Flemish *grande chapelle* and as clavichord teacher for chapel members.[16] Bredemers became one of the highest paid musicians in Charles V's court, traveling with the king around his ever-expanding domains. In 1520 he was with Charles V when he was crowned Holy Roman Emperor in Aachen.

Charles V brought with him, wherever he went, a sense of Flemish art and culture acquired in his aunt Margaret's court. When he married the lovely, intelligent Isabella of Portugal in Valladolid in 1525, she immediately organized her own Spanish "capella." She took into her court the extraordinary composer Antonio de Cabezón as clavichordist and organist. After her death in 1538, Cabezón stayed on as Charles's chamber musician, remaining with him his entire reign.

Meanwhile, Charles V went on to amass territories across Europe as well as in the Far East, Africa, and America. Lavish masses and motets praised him as a Roman Catholic ruler-conqueror who sought to save the world from Protestants, Turks, Incas, and Aztecs. Spain itself not only replaced Flanders as a powerful center for the arts but also produced one of the major mystic writers of all times in Saint Theresa of Ávila.

Philip II (1527–1598)

In the end Charles V retired to a monastery. He left his son Philip to keep spreading the magnificence of the Spanish Habsburg Empire.

Spain

Antonio de Cabezón (1510–1566)

Philip II studied the clavichord in his youth. His teacher was Antonio de Cabezón, the great Spanish clavichord and organ composer-performer. In 1543, when Philip II was made regent of Spain, this blind musician became his court organist. As a member of the Spanish capella, Cabezón traveled with Philip to the Netherlands, Italy, Germany, and England.

Thus in both the reigns of Charles V and Philip II, Cabezón was a vital part of Spain's artistic Golden Era. Certainly his *diferencias* and *tientos* can be profoundly beautiful when played on the clavichord.[17]

Tomás de Santa María (c. 1510–1570)

Friar Santa María's book *Libro llamado Arte de tãner Fantasia* (The art of playing the fantasia) received Cabezón's approval on its title page. This extensive treatise on sixteenth-century keyboard music (1541–65) discusses the clavichord specifically. No Spanish clavichord however, of this period survives.

Santa Maria describes a lost way of playing the clavichord that may seem difficult and strange. Keep your mind open while you attempt it.[18] A detail from a Portuguese monastery (found in Brauchli's book) gives you a visual idea of his directions, paraphrased here:

1. Crook your hand like a cat's paw and curl your fingers so that they arch well above your hand.
   - The more your fingers are flexed like a bow, the stronger the attack and the fuller, more lively, and brilliant the sound.

2. Contract your hand, keeping fingers 2345 close together.
   - Finger 5 is so contracted that it almost touches the palm.
   - Your thumb lies limp and much lower when not in use. Its outermost joint bends toward the palm so that it can move easily under your arched hand.
   - If you spread out your fingers, your hand will lose its power.

3. Keep the wrists lower than the hands.
   - Do not lift the palm when striking the keys.
   - Strike with the balls of your fingertips, extending the fingers forward.
   - The touch will be mellow, since the fleshy part of the finger is soft.

4. To release a key, raise the finger slightly upward.
   - If you push the finger away or bend it under, you will make noise on the key.

5. For repeated notes using two fingers, turn your arm sideways, parallel to the width of the keyboard, "so that the arm, from elbow to fingers, is over the clavichord."[19]

Certain rules of Santa María will seem more natural to you:

- Play from key level and close to the key ends.
- If you press the strings too far, the pitch will sharpen.
- If you slacken the pressure, the sound will weaken.
- To give clarity, lift one finger before the next one strikes, or the sounds will overlap and blur.

Concerning fingering, Santa María believed it is ultimately up to the player. However, he gives a number of possibilities that include the modern 54321321 on eighth notes, right hand descending. Most of the examples given here will be new to you. Remember to keep your thumb very low and your three middle fingers over the keys. Examples 7.4 and 7.5 show whole and half notes and then quarter notes in the right hand.

EXAMPLE 7.4

EXAMPLE 7.5

Santa María gives an unusually practical explanation on how to maneuver fingers in quarter-note runs. It is worthwhile to try his instructions, since they may be applied to other situations.

Example 7.6 shows a run of quarter notes for the left hand. Since finger 3 is longer and stronger, it is placed higher and farther from the key end than fingers 2 and 4. The latter fingers, lifted only slightly, appear to creep along the extreme near ends of the keys. (Remember to slant your hand in the direction of the run.) Again, the longer finger (2 ascending or 3 descending) is placed higher up the key than the other finger (1 ascending or 4 descending), which seems to crawl along the ends of the keys.

EXAMPLE 7.6

Santa María is one of the few to discuss rhythmic inequality in keyboard music.[20] He possibly coordinated this inequality with his choice of fingerings. The effect itself, however, may be more of a lilt than a rigid difference in note values. The first line of example 7.7 shows the music as it is written on the page. The second line shows how the first and third notes can be held a little longer, while the second and fourth notes are slightly hurried.

EXAMPLE 7.7

In elegant, brief *glosas* (i.e., Spanish ornamental lines), the first and third notes are hurried instead, and the second and fourth are prolonged (example 7.8).

EXAMPLE 7.8

For the most elegant long and short *glosas,* the first three eighth notes are hurried, and the fourth is lengthened. The next downbeat, however, must be on time.

Italy

Girolamo Diruta (c. 1554–after 1610)

Girolamo Diruta, a Franciscan monk of the generation following Santa María, criticizes the latter's hand position in *Il Transilvano,* part 1 (1593). He strongly objects to the crippling effect of hiding the thumbs and fifth fingers and holding the arms so low that the hands seem to hang from the keys.

Although Diruta concentrates on the organ, he lived at a time when Italian clavichords were still being built and played. In fact, clavichord technique is particularly helpful for playing sixteenth-century Italian organs that are delicately voiced on low wind pressure. Thus the following paraphrase of Diruta's instructions is useful for the clavichord and seems more natural today than Santa María's approach.

1. Do not twist about like a comedian but stay quietly at the keyboard.
2. Raise your wrist very slightly so that your hand and forearm are in a straight line.
3. Cup your hand by drawing in your fingers so that the hand is arched and the fingers are curved.
4. Rest your hand lightly on the keyboard as if caressing and charming a child.
5. Let your arm guide your hand while your fingers lie evenly on the keys.
6. Fingers become quick and agile. Sounds are pleasant and sweet.

England

In 1554 young Philip II of Spain became king of England when, for political reasons, he married Queen Mary I. The composer Cabezón was among the musicians who traveled with Philip. When Mary died four years later, Philip II proposed marriage, unsuccessfully, to her younger half-sister, Queen Elizabeth I (1533–1603).

Spanish and English musical practices show similarities in the sixteenth century. In both countries keyboard variations, imitating the lute and guitar, involve embroidered melodies over a repeated pattern in the bass.

Excellent English keyboard music of the sixteenth and seventeenth centuries may be found in large manuscript collections, such as the so-called *Fitzwilliam Virginal Book.* Taking into account that the title of this manuscript was added later, some of this music seems delightfully suitable to the clavichord.[21] (The word "virginal" was added after the Elizabethan era.)[22]

John Bull (c. 1562–1628)

John Bull taught Elizabeth I before she became queen. She greatly admired his music, and some say she also used him for foreign espionage. The variations found in his grounds are distant relations to Cabezón's *diferencias.*

The *Fitzwilliam Book* is filled with music by John Bull as well as Giles Farnaby and William Byrd. An excerpt from Bull's partly fingered prelude is included as example 7.9.[23] Playing these measures nonlegato and repeating them offers you excellent training for the clavichord.[24] The more you feel at home with premodern fingering, the more flexible and adaptable your fingers will be.

EXAMPLE 7.9 John Bull, prelude

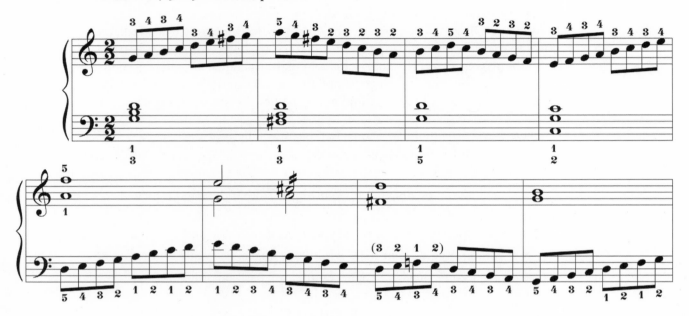

In 1613 Bull fled to Flanders, ostensibly because of his seduction of maidens and married ladies. He likely encountered the famed Dutch organist Jan Pieterszoon Sweelinck (1562–1621), whose unpedaled keyboard music may be played on the clavichord.

France

Emperor Charles V's sister Eleanor, a student of Bredemers, was admired for her passionate clavichord playing. In 1530 she married King Francis I of France, who kept a brilliant court of musicians, artists, poets, and savants. Within a year, Pierre Attaignant began publishing in Paris a series of volumes in tablature containing dances, chansons, and religious music "for organs, spinets, clavichords and similar instruments."[25] By 1537 he had been appointed Francis I's royal printer.

Eleanor's marriage was intended to soothe the bitter rivalry between Charles V and Francis I. Over a century would go by, however, until finally French royalty would supersede the Spanish Habsburgs.

France became Europe's dominant power during the long, flamboyant reign of King Louis XIV (1638–1715). The king's lavish style flourished as the model at foreign courts. In music, dance, art, architecture, and philosophy, France offered a new life to the culture of Europe.

Jacques Champion de Chambonnières (1601/2–1672)

In early seventeenth-century France, clavichords were well on the wane, although they were still being built and played. Marin Mersenne describes a clavichord of four complete octaves and provides a drawing in his treatise *Harmonie universelle,* book 3 (Paris, 1636). From then on France's effect on the clavichord appears to be indirect.

When Louis XIV became child-king in 1643, his regent mother (a descendant of Emperor Maximilian) provided him with a harpsichord. This brilliantly colorful, light-keyed instrument was more suited to French etiquette than the clavichord. It replaced the lute at court, with Chambonnières as its main artist. This composer, an excellent dancer, also appeared with young Louis XIV in private court performances. Thus both lute and dance inspired Chambonnières to imbue his keyboard music with a new elegance. His subtle use of the lute's *style brisé* (broken chords and voice lines) and his delicate *jeu coulant* (flowing style) would take him as far away as Sweden.

Chambonnières, however, rarely played a piece the same way twice. Only in his last years did he pen two books of highly expressive music, published in 1670.[26] A few measures of one allemande appear in example 7.10.

EXAMPLE 7.10   Jacques Champion de Chambonnières, allemande

Guillaume-Gabriel Nivers (1632–1714)

Nivers, a probable student of Chambonnières, was organist for Saint-Sulpice in Paris and music master for the king's wife. The following words from Nivers's *Livre d'orgue* (1665) are broad enough to be applied to the clavichord.

1. Play effortlessly by placing your fingers on the keyboard gracefully and evenly.
   - Longer fingers are curved to be in line with shorter ones.
   - Lift each note promptly as you play the next. If you wait until after the next is played, you confuse rather than distinguish the notes.
   - To connect notes, you still distinguish them, but the notes are not released so promptly.
2. In elegant playing, all notes are distinct, and some are slightly slurred. This is best learned from singing.

Germanic Countries

Johann Jacob Froberger (1616–1667)

In Germanic countries, interest in the clavichord would grow rather than die away as it had in France. One of the finest of keyboard composers, Froberger, wrote music that is ideal for the clavichord. However, Froberger did not limit his outlook to Germany. In his youth, he encountered foreign musicians in the court at Stuttgart. Later he spent years in Vienna and studied with Frescobaldi in Rome. As a keyboardist, he was deeply affected by France.

In 1652 Froberger arrived in Paris during the early years of Louis XIV's reign. Inspired by harpsichordists like Chambonnières and French lutenists like Denis Gaultier, Froberger combined their elegant *style brisé* with German introspection and Italian emotional drama. His tragic tombeaux and laments and his sensitive dance suites are particularly exquisite on the clavichord since they lend themselves to subtle dynamic shading.

Froberger gave descriptive titles to the free, programmatic pieces composed around the time he lived in Paris. For his famous "Tombeau fait à Paris sur la mort de Monsieur Blanceroche," he states that it should be performed "very slowly, as seen fit, without observing any measured time" (fort lentement à la discretion sans observer aucune mesure).[27]

A similar emotional, descriptive work by Froberger is "Plainte faite a Londres pour passer la melancholi." This "Lament composed in London to overcome melancholy" exists only in a hastily written Viennese manuscript that also describes the story in Latin. It claims that while traveling from Paris to England, Froberger was robbed at sea between Calais and Dover. Penniless, he landed in England in a fishing boat. After setting out for London, each time he wanted to join a group to hear organ music, he was obliged to operate the bellows. Once when in his melancholy he forgot to work them, the organist kicked him out the door.[28]

The drama is most apparent in the second half of this piece, shown in example 7.11. The rise and fall of thirty-second notes, irregular timing, and strong cadence suggest Froberger's harsh exit. Finally, the last four softer measures, with their plaintively hesitant *stile brisé,* suggest the composer sadly continuing on his way.

EXAMPLE 7.11 Johann Jacob Froberger, "Plainte faite a Londres pour passer la melancholi"

Froberger was a great influence on his colleague and friend Louis Couperin, known for his amazing unmeasured preludes. Although few of Froberger's keyboard works were published in his lifetime, handwritten copies circulated in various European countries. He became an important part of the tradition that led to the music of Johann Sebastian Bach.

According to Emanuel Bach, his father loved and studied Froberger's music.[29] In fact, interest in this composer continued throughout the eighteenth century. Beethoven was acquainted with his work, and Mozart penned copies of his *Hexachord Fantasia* that still survive today.

Johann Caspar Ferdinand Fischer (1656–1746)

The effect of French music on Germanic composers can be found later in works such as those by Johann Caspar Ferdinand Fischer. Born in Bohemia and influenced by Lully, he wrote delicate suites of considerable beauty. With the coming of well-tempered tunings, he presaged Johann Sebastian Bach in composing preludes and fugues for a sequence of major and minor keys.

Fischer served for many years as Kapellmeister to Ludwig Wilhelm, margrave of Baden-Baden. On the birth of the margrave's son in 1698, Fischer presented the margravine with a set of delightful suites called *Musicalisches Blumen-Büschlein* (Little musical bouquet).

The second suite contains a *passacaille* that opens as shown in example 7.12.[30] This entire suite may be played on a portable clavichord of four octaves, possibly with a short octave in the bass.[31]

EXAMPLE 7.12   Johann Caspar Ferdinand Fischer, *passacaille*

This music is not meant for display. In keeping with the clavichord, it is intended for innocent pleasure within the intimacy of a noble home. In a rare mention of this instrument, Fischer wrote in his dedication, "So as not to harm the tender ears of the new-born prince . . . this is gentle music, to be played on the clavichord alone."[32]

CHAPTER EIGHT

Exploring Eighteenth-Century Germany

COMPARED TO FRANCE during the eighteenth century, Germany was fragmented, with no central church or central king to dictate musical tastes. Lutherans, abandoning the pope, preferred a more personal relationship with Jesus and God. Perhaps it was Johann Sebastian Bach himself who wrote in a 1738 thoroughbass primer: "The final purpose of all music . . . is nothing other than the praise of God and the re-creation of the soul. Where this is not taken into account, then there is no true music, only a devilish bawling and droning."[1]

The following generation, affected by German Enlightenment and the sentimentality of Pietism, focused on expressing a wider range of human emotions. While François Couperin in France might strive to notate a precise portraiture of a feeling, it was essential for a German keyboardist to express a feeling freshly each time it was conveyed. This was accomplished mainly through delicate shading, for which the clavichord proved to be the ideal instrument. Thus it flourished in the period of *Empfindsamkeit* (expressiveness) and, along with the fortepiano, in the more dramatic period of *Sturm und Drang* (storm and stress).

J. S. Bach wrote few dynamic markings, and these were directed toward degrees of softening the sound. In Emanuel's time, the keyboard crescendo was extended through dynamic-rich clavichords and the first fortepianos with their slightly louder tones. In the sweep of the entire century, some of the most famous Germanic composers played four- and five-octave clavichords along with the fortepiano and its changing forms.

Johann Sebastian Bach (1685–1750)

Bach is said to have expressed his "most refined thoughts" on the clavichord. He preferred it to the harpsichord because the latter lacked sufficient "soul."[2]

Since many capable authors have written about Bach and his keyboard music, this chapter will touch on only two topics. The first, French dance, has greatly affected the playing of modern keyboardists; the second, Bach's use of fingering, is still neglected today.[3]

Bach was intimately acquainted with German music of earlier generations and likewise with the music of Italy and France. Although he never traveled outside of Germany, Bach heard French musicians from the time of his youth. He became acquainted with Louis XIV's court dances and dance music in vogue among German nobility and the educated middle class. In fact, the king of Saxony's French dance masters and virtuoso musicians numbered among Bach's friends.

Bach was known to have admired the charm and elegance of French keyboard music. He knew the suites of François Couperin, famed harpsichordist and composer in Louis XIV's court for many years. Likewise, he profited from *L'art de toucher le clavecin* (*The Art of Playing the Harpsichord,* 1716 and revised and corrected in 1717), which showed how Couperin wanted his music played. Fingering, touch, and precision of ornamentation are included in this book. Thus, French music "was an intrinsic, important and graceful component of Bach's world." In fact, certain Bach dances played on the clavichord can reflect "the noble and subtle movements of early ballet."[4]

Conceiving a specific dance on the clavichord, however, involves more than playing quickly with a snappy staccato. Each dance has its own pattern and meaning. By studying, watching, or actually dancing a simple form of a dance, you will discover details of articulation and phrasing that give this music life.[5]

At the beginning of the notebook Bach gave his wife, the singer Anna Magdalena, he penned his own "French" Suites. Later, Anna Magdalena copied in her book a French *rondeau* that starts with the measures shown in example 8.1.

EXAMPLE 8.1 *Rondeau* from *Little Notebook for Anna Magdalena Bach*

Couperin composed an earlier version of the *rondeau* in his descriptive piece "Les bergeries" (The sheepfolds) (example 8.2). Notice how this French version is much more nuanced in detail than the German version. It shows in the left hand a complex overlapping of notes, while in the right hand, a variety of ornamental signs invite intricate timing.

EXAMPLE 8.2 François Couperin, *rondeau* "Les bergeries" (The sheepfolds)

Bach was a master at bringing out the meaning of each voice on a clavier (or keyboard instrument) and combining contrapuntal voices as a whole. Thumbs and their flexibility became extremely important. According to those who admired him, "All his fingers were equally skillful; all were capable of the most perfect accuracy in performance." He could "conquer the greatest difficulties with the most flowing ease."[6]

As a teacher, Bach started clavier students with exercises for all ten fingers, emphasizing the production of clear, singing tones (see chapter 3). Students had to continue these exercises while adding small example pieces that employed their fingers in various ways. For this, the clavichord was particularly useful as a beginner's instrument since it reflected the slightest inequality or uncertainly of tone.

One important element in Bach's playing needs attention today. When using modern fingering only, we limit our understanding of his music. Hence it is helpful to play the few of his fingerings that still exist. At the same time, these fingerings are not meant to clumsily link notes by pairs or suggest a sterile, unbroken staccato line. Rather, the various articulations, dynamics, and inflections can give a piece character, breath, and momentum.

A rare example of Bach's fingering is found in "Applicatio" from the *Clavier-Büchlein* for Wilhelm Friedemann, Bach's student and eldest son. In the top voice, Bach indicated the old 343434(5) fingering in ascent and "modern" fingering in descent. In the third measure only, the old 3212121 ascends in the bass (example 8.3). Later, when Wilhelm Friedemann became a famous organist, he was admired for his amazingly smooth and rapid runs using only two fingers.[7]

Bach began his son's little clavier book in 1720. Within the next few years, he made collections of his teaching pieces. They included his contrapuntal two-part inventions and three-part sinfonias, his "English" and "French" Suites, and the first book of *The Well-Tempered Clavier*. In these works, which sound so beautiful on the clavichord, there are places where Bach's "Applicatio" fingering may be applied.

Play "Applicatio" slowly, one voice at a time. Omit the ornaments and dwell on the fingerings that seem unusual to you. Be conscious of possible articulations or shifting of the entire hand. Note the thumb's prominence in the middle voice of the final measure. Finally, play all the voices together.

EXAMPLE 8.3   Johann Sebastian Bach, "Applicatio," in *Clavier-Büchlein vor Wilhelm Friedemann Bach*

"Applicatio" is also a training tool for ornaments, which Bach believed should be practiced from the beginning. Four ornaments from the table he wrote for Wilhelm Friedemann are given in example 8.4. Techniques for playing them may be found in chapter 5 of this book.

EXAMPLE 8.4

The only other direct source of Bach's fingering is his Praeambulum in G Minor (BWV 930), also found in Wilhelm Friedemann's little book. Example 8.5 provides a few measures of this piece.

EXAMPLE 8.5   Johann Sebastian Bach, Praeambulum in G Minor (BWV 930), in *Clavier-Büchlein vor Wilhelm Friedemann Bach*

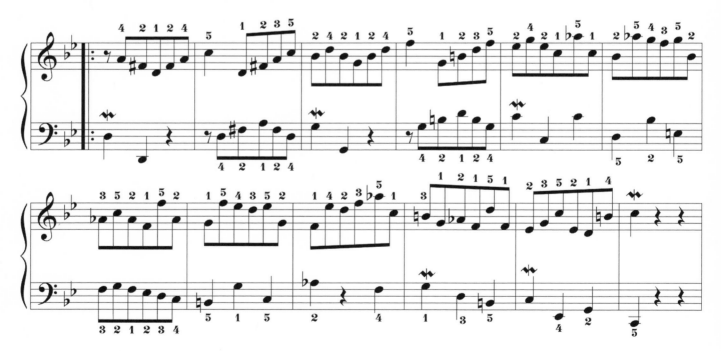

One secondary source of Bach fingering is found in an early version of the first prelude from *The Well-Tempered Clavier,* Book II. This "Prelude composée par J. S. Bach" (BWV 870a) was copied by Johann Caspar Vogler, young Bach's gifted pupil from 1710 to 1715. The last measures are shown in example 8.6.

EXAMPLE 8.6   Johann Sebastian Bach, "Prelude composée par J. S. Bach" (BWV 870a)

Occasionally, as with Couperin, several successive notes are played with a single fifth finger (soprano, mm. 1 and 2) or a thumb (tenor, mm. 3 and 4). In measure 3 (beginning with bass C on the second beat) the fingering 545 suggests a lateral shift of the whole hand to the right. This encourages a slight emphasis on beat 3. Since this four-voiced selection is difficult, simply study it one voice at a time. Be sure to relax the thumb when it is not in use.

Bach teaches us mainly through his music.[8] In his later years he left it to his son Emanuel to write down how the clavier was to be played. Emanuel credited his father for the fingerings in part 1 of his *Essay* (1753).

Carl Philipp Emanuel Bach (1714–1788)

Emanuel Bach is considered to be one of the finest and most expressive clavichord composer-performers of all time. As a child, he had the privilege of studying with his father. From 1740 to 1767 he served Prussia's Frederick the Great, mainly as cembalist for the king's nightly flute performances. Emanuel was one of the chief proponents of the German Enlightenment, in contrast with the Francophile King Frederick, who liked to consider himself an enlightened but autocratic king. In his latter years Emanuel lived in Hamburg as a free, cultured man who served as musical director of the Protestant Michaeliskirche.

In 1773 Charles Burney, the English writer, visited Emanuel and wrote later:

> Mr. Bach was so obliging as to sit down to his Silbermann clavichord and favorite instrument upon which he played three or four of his choicest and most difficult composition with the delicacy, precision and spirit for which he is so justly celebrated. . . . After dinner, which was elegantly served and cheerfully eaten, I prevailed upon him to sit down again to a clavichord, and he played, with little intermission till near eleven o'clock at night. During this time, he grew so animated and *possessed* that he not only played but looked like one inspired. His eyes were fixed, his under lip fell and drops of effervescence distilled from his countenance.[9]

Emanuel was a superb teacher. Like Couperin and Quantz before him, he influenced many students with his instruction book of 1753.[10] An immediate success, it was followed by a second part printed in 1762. Later, Emanuel wrote, "I have observed, with the greatest satisfaction, the change that has come over the world of clavier playing since the publication of my *Essay*."[11]

Emanuel's work influenced Mozart and Haydn in Austria and reached as far as Russia and Sweden. Both Beethoven and Czerny used the *Essay* in their teaching. Certainly his book, if absorbed bit by bit, is essential for all keyboardists playing eighteenth-century music today.

Among the famous remarks he made on the importance of expressive playing are the following:

1. "Keyboardists whose chief asset is mere technique . . . astound us with their prowess without ever touching our sensibilities. They overwhelm our hearing without satisfying it and stun the mind without moving it. . . . A mere technician, however, can lay no claim to the rewards of those who sway in gentle undulation the ear rather than the eye, the heart rather than the ear, and lead it where they will."[12]

2. "A musician cannot move others unless he too is moved. He must of necessity feel all of the affects that he hopes to arouse in his audience, for the revealing of his own feeling will stimulate a like feeling in the listener. In languishing, sad passages, the performer must languish and grow sad. Thus will the expression of the piece be more clearly perceived by the audience."[13]

3. "It is especially in fantasias, those expressive not of memorized or plagiarized passages, but rather of true, musical creativeness, that the keyboardist . . . can practice the declamatory style, and move audaciously from one affect to another."[14]

The first chapter of the *Essay* is devoted to proper fingering. Emanuel said it is "inseparably related to the whole art of performance." He felt that "more is lost through poor fingering than can be replaced by all conceivable artistry and good taste."[15] During his lifetime, with the advent of the five-octave clavichord, Emanuel extended "modern" scale fingering beyond the octave. This encouraged a sweep of scale passages, particularly in his fantasias, that presaged their expressive use in the romantic era.

From his father, Emanuel learned the "secret" of making the thumb a principal finger in order to sustain and contour each voice and to play in all keys. What we accept today as natural seemed in his Germany excitingly new: make the thumb a pivot, turning it under the middle fingers or crossing those fingers over it; then "the tones involved in the change flow smoothly."[16] According to Emanuel, when the thumb "has learned to turn and take its note automatically," the player has "gained the summit of fingering."[17]

Only in the eighteenth century, when equal tunings made this possible, did clavier music include all twenty-four scales. Emanuel was among the first to advise practicing each one of them. For scales with more sharps and flats, he applied this easy rule: the thumb is best used before or after raised keys, for then it has more space in which to move. Thus, for the most remote keys, modern fingering was the logical choice.

For common scales with few raised keys, however, Emanuel offered more than one solution. On the C major scale in example 8.7, he placed his first choice closest to the notes. He favored modern fingering except in the bass descending, where 12341234 is preferred. Although still popular in 1753, the old 12343434 and 43212121 fingerings were Emanuel's second choice, except in the bass ascending, where they were his third.

EXAMPLE 8.7

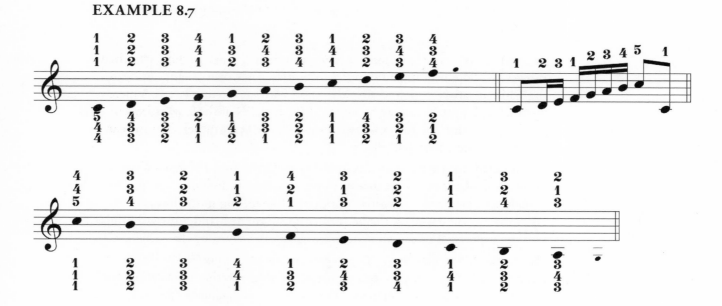

Fingerings 343434 and 212121 had been used since the time of Santa María. Thus, of all "old" fingerings, these are the most important to practice until they seem natural. Examples 8.8 and 8.9 show these two fingerings using the C major scale.

EXAMPLE 8.8

EXAMPLE 8.9

To supplement part 1 of his *Essay* (1753), Emanuel fingered eighteen *Probestücke* (example pieces) and arranged them into six sonatas. It can be both fascinating and rewarding to study these pieces, searching for the reasons for their fingering as if on a musical treasure hunt.

The sixteenth "example piece," the Fantasia in C Minor (the only fantasia he ever fingered), displays Emanuel's expressive abilities at their best. Absence of bar lines in the outer sections encourages fluctuations in tempo and meter to show gradual or sudden shifts of emotion. Expanding, irregular phrases and extensive dynamic shading allow the music to breathe like a singer. All these qualities suited Emanuel's famed Silbermann clavichord, which was capable of expressing emotions ranging from a whisper to a cry.

Like the coloratura singers of his day, Emanuel did not use an extended legato for dramatic lines. Rather, his fingerings suggest subtle breaks of sound that convey expressive details without ever losing the music's momentum. These emotional coloratura-like passages in the soprano are either supported by fingered broken chords in the bass or left to soar freely over silence.

Example 8.10 shows the first third of the Fantasia in C Minor.

EXAMPLE 8.10   C. P. E. Bach, Fantasia in C Minor

The following analysis of the relationship of fingering to music applies to the first part of Emanuel's extraordinary fantasia. Lowercase letters in parentheses refer to locations on its printed page.

(a) On the second bass C of the opening arpeggio, finger 5 is substituted for finger 1. This emphasizes the C without breaking the arpeggio's upward extension. It positions the hand so the C minor chord can resonate longer than a whole note. Consequently, the music is grounded in C minor and yet directed toward the treble.

(b) Finger 5 on F is followed by 3 on E♭. This positions the hand so it is easy for fingers 2 and 5 to play D and A♭. Note that the sixteenth notes have more rhythmic freedom when the bass is resting.

(c) Finger 2 releases the last slurred sixteenth note C a little early. Then the second C, as a half note, is played with finger 5. The necessary shift of the whole hand helps emphasize the second C, particularly if the fifth finger-tip is in a strong position to catch and hold the key. In this way, the sound will carry as a suspension against the new intensely dissonant diminished seventh chord over a C pedal tone in the bass.

(d) Finger 5 plays four treble notes in a row, since the other fingers are occupied with a held diminished chord. C and B♮, covered by a slur, can give the effect of being connected by moving the fifth finger very adroitly. Thus, a highly flexible but strong finger 5 can shape the suspension, including its rest, and final resolution.

(e) F is played with finger 2 and then finger 4. This requires the same hand shift to the second note as in (c) above. It also prepares for the proper fingering of the coming arpeggio. Note in the bass how C finally resolves to B♮ for the diminished seventh chord.

(f) This is the first of three related extensions of the diminished chord in the treble. It is easy to play two fifth fingers in a row: the A♭ is released after the slur, and G is brought out as an appoggiatura ending with a pianissimo.

(g) The second extension expands by starting out in *forte* triplets, accentuated by the fingering, and going up as far as a slurred appoggiatura on C to B♮. The intensity rises in the treble while the bass is silent.

(h) The third extension starts with a loud rush of sixteenth notes. A repeated 321 finger pattern plays against the meter to heighten the tension and drive the line upward. Absence of a bass gives the soprano line freedom to expand from B♮, finally breaking loose from the diminished seventh on a high B♭.

(i) The fingering continues in threes, slower paced and descending, to follow the scale of C minor down to, finally, C.

(j) A repeat of the low bass C of the very beginning brings a closure to these first lines of the fantasia.

(k) The mood shifts abruptly with a run in thirty-second notes made easier by modern fingering, with the thumb kept for lower keys.

(l) The run pattern and fingering are repeated five notes lower in octaves. This time there is a D♭ included to make a transition to the chord of A♭ major.

(m) The soprano solos with a series of two slurred notes, fingered accordingly.

(n) The second A♭ arpeggio in the bass starts one sixty-fourth note late, as does the soprano, which runs quickly up the A♭ scale in sixty-fourth notes, again using modern fingering. The line slows down with four descending eighth notes, reinforced by the sign of a *portato.* They lead into a diminished chord on A♭, with a suspension from E♭ resolving to E♮.

Subsequent changes in harmony, not shown here, are excitingly unusual for the mid-eighteenth century. In fact, this very fantasia gained immediate fame as an example of Emanuel's astounding clavichord improvisations.

Emanuel recognized the importance of listening to fine singers, but he developed his own style of adapting drama to the keyboard. His friend the poet and playwright Heinrich Wilhelm von Gerstenberg combined this fantasia with the sung words of Hamlet's "To be or not to be, that is the great question." The placement of syllables, as seen in the Fantasia in C Minor, suggests, perhaps, how the work may have been played. Von Gerstenberg's version was published only in 1787, thirty-four years after Emanuel's *Probestücke.*

Except for the *Probestücke,* most of Emanuel's keyboard music is not fingered.[18] Of particular interest are his *6 Sonatine nuove (Sechs neue Clavierstücke).* They were published for the new edition of his *Essay* in Hamburg in 1787, the year before he died. One of these short pieces is shown for you to play in example 8.11.

EXAMPLE 8.11 (*facing*)   C. P. E. Bach, Allegretto, from *6 Sonatine nuove*

Daniel Gottlob Türk (1750–1813)

Türk championed the clavichord into the nineteenth century and praised it as ideal for beginners. "On no other keyboard instrument is it possible," he wrote, to play with such "finesse."[19] In Halle, Türk was admired as a teacher of children and university students. According to one pupil, he showed how to "coax sounds" out of the clavichord rather than to "pound them out, as is so common today."[20]

Türk's own training had been under Johann Sebastian's pupils in Dresden and Leipzig. Later he collected and crafted basic material that complemented Emanuel Bach's more advanced *Essay*. Türk's *School of Clavier Playing* was published in 1789, the year after Emanuel Bach's death. The book is particularly appealing because it specifically addresses the needs of a clavichord beginner.

In his first lessons, Türk focuses on the sustained touch and supple, singing tone described earlier in this book. He starts with the slow and attentive practice of a series of long, single notes. Keys should be struck moderately and then pressed down so the tone reaches its maximum strength without raising the pitch. The very beginner, concentrating on this tonal control, should practice only about six hours a week.[21] To quicken progress, Türk suggests the concurrent study of flute, violin, and voice. Later the beginner can sing simple songs with the clavichord, such as J. F. Reichhardt's *Lieder für Kinder*.

According to Türk, the ideal clavichord has five octaves, a long-lasting tone, a wide dynamic range, and a vibrato that can be "clearly heard."[22] Like the ever-expanding fortepiano, the clavichord fulfilled the growing emotional demands of keyboard music. "The better the instrument," Türk claimed, "the greater the gain for the pupil, for he will . . . learn to play with more expression than he would by having to pound on a miserable old box, as is often the case."[23]

Türk impressed his students with his own expressive playing and the excellent fingerings he provided. *School of Clavier Playing* offers many interesting pages on fingering, including some difficult hand-crossing examples by J. S. Bach and his sons as well as Haydn and Hässler. Here are a few student topics Türk addresses:

1. To play in a "well-grounded and free-flowing manner," fingering should be comfortable and natural.[24] Use the minimum amount of hand motion, and stay free of any "old entrenched habits."[25]

2. The beginner's custom of pushing down a key with two fingers is incorrect. "A clavichord hardly requires such strength, even for a child."[26] If the action is unusually stiff, then find another clavichord.

3. The thumb is more important than the fifth finger. Do not neglect it and leave it hanging or let it interrupt the music's flow. Instead, use it particularly before and after raised keys.

4. Practice bending the thumb gradually under the other fingers and crossing them over it until this makes no difference in the sound. There should be no break in the legato and no twisting of the fingers and hands. The thumb should arrive on its next key just in time to play it.[27]

5. For the beginner, scale practice is the foundation of all fingering. In a number of cases Türk offers more fingering options than Emanuel Bach, though he still does not give set fingerings for every scale. Most of his "preferred" fingerings are in use today.

Like Emanuel Bach, Türk places scale fingering above and below the notes. In the C scale in example 8.12, those fingerings nearest the notes are the ones that he prefers. Notice that the old 343434 and 212121 fingerings Emanuel considered common are now "rare."

EXAMPLE 8.12

When Türk introduces the beginner to very short pieces, he adds the following advice:

1. Take time to be alert to all details.
2. To choose a fingering, look ahead in the music.
3. All fingering should fit the hand and the piece being played.
4. Rarely do two clavichordists—even great ones—use the same fingering throughout a piece.
5. To learn to strike keys correctly without watching, play a memorized piece in the dark.

Like Emanuel Bach, Türk says, "A true musician should . . . respond to all the passions and emotions that can be expressed in music."[28] For each affect, a clavichord player should know when to linger on an important note, hurry unimportant ones, and modify the tone. Thus, for the more advanced clavichord pupil, Türk describes the expressive use of shading, articulation, and timing. He compares the clavichordist to an orator or singer:

1. A selection of music, like a speech, may be divided into larger and smaller parts.
2. The orator emphasizes and lingers on important syllables. The same is true in music. Usually this brief lengthening of a note is scarcely perceptible, and the next note loses an equal amount of value.
3. A clavichordist who divides an idea by interrupting a row of tones improperly is like an orator pausing in the middle of a word to take a breath.
4. More important notes are played longer and louder, while less important ones are quicker and softer, the way a singer would sing these notes or a good orator declaim the words.
5. It is important to listen to singers and players of great sensitivity. Certain subtleties of expression can only be heard.[29]

Türk speaks of tonal shading in detail:

1. *Forte* and *piano* are general terms. Even the most painstaking markings cannot describe the possible gradations of loudness and softness of tone.
2. "The most beautiful tone is one that takes upon itself every mode of expression and, in all the shadings of *forte* and *piano,* remains both clear and bright."[30]
3. A piece of music may be compared to a painting in which certain parts are in shadow and other parts in light.

Türk concludes his book with *Twelve Pieces for Instruction.* Among them is the following delicate "Minuetto." It was written a half century after the minuets in Anna Magdalena Bach's notebook. According to Türk, this piece requires a light style of performance, leaving the key quite quickly and playing the notes less firmly (example 8.13).

EXAMPLE 8.13   Daniel Gottlob Türk, "Minuetto"

The second piece, "Arioso," is to be played slowly and lingeringly in what Türk would call the more sustained style. Each tone has an emphasis, and all slurred notes are to be held throughout their entire duration without the slightest separation (example 8.14).

EXAMPLE 8.14   Daniel Gottlob Türk

A later edition of Türk's *School of Clavier Playing* was published in 1802. Franz Schubert was a child of five, and Felix Mendelssohn (who kept his father's clavichord) would be born in seven years. At this late date Türk still repeated his preference for the clavichord, although he admitted that the piano, too, could produce a supple, singing sound.

Türk's remarkable explanations of shading and timing will help you understand how emotions were expressed on the clavichord in his day. Like Emanuel Bach, he warns against imitating like a trained bird. Rather, he teaches that true expression comes from nuances that are beyond all words.

In conclusion, this chapter offers you, for future playing, the beautiful "Andante ma innocentemente," Emanuel Bach's second example piece for his *Essay on the True Art of Playing Keyboard Instruments* (example 8.15, page 102). The fingerings will give you insights into how to play this music. Note the variations of detachment and connection and the dynamic markings. Remember to lower the key slightly before making a softer tone. Eventually you will find yourself playing subtle inflections on the clavichord spontaneously on your own.

EXAMPLE 8.15   C. P. E. Bach, *Probe-stücken* (1753) no. 2

Andante mà innocentemente

CHAPTER NINE

Exploring the Present and Future

ALTHOUGH THIS CENTURY appears to revel in loud, amplified sound and endless stress, there is a growing need for quietness as a balance. A clavichord can fill this need. Already a century ago, Arnold Dolmetsch stimulated a clavichord revival among a few elite in England and America. He wrote on his Chickering clavichord lids the French proverb "Plus fait douceur que violence" (Sweetness achieves more than violence).

People have been playing the clavichord since the 1400s. In some countries it was fashionable until the late eighteenth century. Then, after a gap in the nineteenth century, when it was abandoned for the piano, it became an instrument for playing music of the past. It is my wish not only that we enjoy this marvelous music on the clavichord but that we widen our horizons to encourage music of our own age as well.

Improvisation

A good clavichord lends itself to improvisation. The tones of this instrument are so subtle and changeable that they can never be repeated exactly the same way. Thus I would encourage all clavichord players to experiment and express themselves with improvisations that are primarily spontaneous and free.

Improvising was an active part of the musical lives of pre-twentieth-century keyboardists. By the sixteenth century, Tomás de Santa María had written a treatise on this art.[1] Later, Mozart, Wilhelm Friedemann Bach, and C. P. E. Bach were famous for their improvisational expertise. The latter wrote a long section on improvisation in part 2 of his *Essay* (1762).[2] He maintained that "it is principally in improvisations or fantasias that the keyboardist can master the feelings of his audience."[3]

In Yogyakarta of the 1980s I visited a venerated old master musician of Java. As I left, I encountered a Greek student who came up to me nearly in tears. It saddened him to realize that students like himself were weakening the oral tradition of Javanese music and stifling it with the printed page. He was aware that this music would lose its improvisational qualities, its alive immediacy, and its un-self-conscious meaning.

My own favorite hour of improvising on the clavichord was at the Zen Mountain Monastery near Woodstock, New York. In the meditation hall, nuns, monks, and laypeople sat on cushions in complete silence. I seemed to breathe in their inner quietness and reflect it back spontaneously in the improvisations that I played.

Ensemble

The pianoforte and clavichord provide the best accompaniments in performances that require the most elegant taste . . . because of the many ways in which their volume can be gradually changed.

C. P. E. Bach, *Essay* (1762)

One tends to think of the soft clavichord as a solo instrument. Yet as early as the fifteenth century an Italian fresco shows one angel strumming the psaltery while two monks play the clavichord and bells. Artworks created in subsequent eras show the lute, recorder, or transverse flute in ensemble with the clavichord. More recently, New York composer David Loeb composed some delicately beautiful music, dedicated to me, for clavichord and shinobue, a high-pitched Japanese transverse flute. In the twenty-first century, the possible combinations that might include the clavichord are endless, particularly in electronic music and other idioms so available to postmodern musicians.

For a Findhorn International Music Festival concert in Scotland, I improvised with vibraphonist Karl Berger of Woodstock fame. Standing before the piano, I used my clavichord technique to create strange tonal textures and rhythmic impulses built on Bach's famous C Major Prelude. Berger spun such a vine of sounds around me that we seemed to dance from the ceiling.

Recordings

Today, via recordings, we have access to an amazing amount of music. We can "hear" clavichordists from all over the world without leaving our homes. Yet interpretations are frozen, and the interaction between performer and listener is lost. Likewise, canned music easily becomes a background for driving on the freeway, doing the dishes, or jogging with the dog. The soft clavichord, in contrast, requires intent listening, and its minute inflections are not easily captured in recording. Yet this medium can offer an enticing introduction to the magic of the clavichord.

Many recordings of clavichord music from the past are available today. Over the last half century the clavichord has been used in a few recordings of popular music. My favorite by far features songs from Gershwin's *Porgy and Bess* turned into delicate improvisations by legendary pianist Oscar Peterson playing the clavichord and Joe Pass playing the acoustic guitar.

Composition for Clavichord and Electronics

In extending electronic music beyond amplified boldness, the clavichord offers much to be explored. In fact, I like to predict that the clavichord will be transformed over time, lending its special capacities to a surprising spectrum of yet-to-exist worlds of sound.

The scene is wide open. So far the emphasis in electronics has been on the loud sounds that amplification encourages. Some forty years ago, when I was a student at the University of Utrecht's Institute of Sonology, teachers were losing their hearing by raising the amp to detect small details on their electronic tapes. (They all wondered what a woman was doing in the class!)

Danger lurks. In my own performance of clavichord with electronic orchestra, I walked out on the stage to find overbearing speakers facing the audience. My clavichord playing, lost in the mix, was inaudible. In contrast, during an online rehearsal, using a piped-in clavichord via the Internet, an explosion of sound shocked the entire building. People came running to the rescue. Even more shocking to them was learning that a clavichord was to blame. Experimental amplification had greatly magnified its tones.

But what about taking electronic music in the other direction—toward the quiet side? The clavichord (unamplified or barely amplified) offers a path back to something society has lost. An interest in finding it again might encourage electronic compositions of a different kind.

The composer John Chowning once commented that the former primacy of auditory experience differs from today. When the sun goes down, ears are no longer making our decisions because we have artificial illumination. Yet our "apparatus" is still with us. We are extremely sensitive to small stuff—echo-location, night noises, our own body sounds. "Free time" away from loudness is nearly nonexistent.

People of all ages, including children, are oblivious to many sounds around them since they are preoccupied with personal electronic devices. Like the average synthesizer, these tend to be limited to a small, blunt range of sound possibilities that can dull even a child's sensitivity to tone.

There is a new wave of electronic companies concentrating on making synthesizers and other instruments with a more detailed range of musical expression. This bodes well for an opening for the clavichord in the twenty-first century. Already elements of the clavichord have been applied to fine synthesizers either by design or by coincidence. For example, the finger *Bebung* that distinguishes the clavichord from all other keyboards has been reinvented as synthesizer "after-touch." The difference today is that finger pressure at the bottom of the key bed is programmable not only as a vibrato but also for other possible tonal modulations. Soft electronic sounds, however, are rare, and usually they are relegated to "meditative music," lacking a complete emotional range.

With Chris Chafe of Stanford's Center for Computer Research in Music and Acoustics (CCRMA) I discussed the need for the clavichord in electronic music to awaken composers to soft and subtle sounds and their manipulation.

At Stanford, Chris placed me on the sole seat in the middle of an amazing, soundproof room. Metal meshing was open below me, and I was surrounded by fourteen sensitive speakers. For the first time, at my request as a clavichordist, the volume was set very low. Waves of soft, exquisitely detailed sounds of great beauty gave me a taste of what superb electronics might produce. Clearly, soft electronic sounds can have a great value of their own.

In a concert Chris and I gave together, electronic music performers and students were astounded and inspired by the soft, tapered sounds they heard. Chafe had composed something he considered the softest piece of computer music ever made. It was ear-opening.

Keeping this in mind, it is clear that playing the clavichord could give one a sense of touch and sound that would expand the possibilities of electronic music. It could even be applied to the new flat-surface instruments regulated by finger touch or any of a number of designs in the field of new instruments for musical expression (NIME). Likewise, natural clavichord sounds could be altered by electronic means, or the instrument itself can be changed dramatically. The following ideas come to mind:

- Expand, contract, or rearrange recorded clavichord sounds electronically.
- Use Internet music transmission, bringing together a clavichord in one part of the world with another quiet instrument in, say, Japan.
- Distort clavichord sound through various manipulations involving reverberation, pitch change, and dynamics.
- Work with envelopes (the shape of a note's attack and delay) and play with filtering for expressive shading and nuances of overtones.
- Improvise electronically in real time with sounds and gestures of a live clavichord picked up via sensors (electronic attachments to capture motions or sound).

I can also imagine a new kind of clavichord capable of entirely fresh dimensions. The modulating touch of finger on key and tangent on string would make tiny, amazing shifts and slides in timbre and pitch. New shadings and articulations would form soft tonal paintings in ways not yet conceived.

This expansion of possibilities for the clavichord will inevitably lead to new techniques. Here, too, the exercises of this book are relevant. They develop that sensitivity to touch and tone so essential to the clavichordist in playing music of the past as well as the future.

Appendix: Biographical Details

About the Author

Joan Benson is one of the foremost clavichordists of modern times. She has been a leading pioneer in promoting the clavichord as a concert instrument, performing in concert halls, universities, and museums around the world. She has taught on the faculty at Stanford University, the University of Oregon, and the Aston Magna Academy in Massachusetts. Her international master classes have introduced many enthusiastic students to the clavichord.

As a child in New Orleans, Benson attended the first progressive school in the Deep South, which stimulated her talent for the arts. She heard Sergei Rachmaninoff and Ignace Paderewski perform and studied with the composer-pianist Percy Grainger.

In her early twenties, while an Indiana University student, Benson received the Kate Neal Kinley International Award for "outstanding powers of artistic communication." She became a protégée of the great Swiss pianist Edwin Fischer, who also taught Alfred Brendel and Paul Badura-Skoda. As a concert pianist her affinity for highly nuanced, gentle, and delicate piano tones, for which she received critical praise, led naturally to her discovery of the clavichord.

After three years of clavichord study with Fritz Neumeyer in Germany and Santiago Kastner in Portugal, Benson returned to the United States to join the faculty of Stanford University. *Saturday Review* selected her first recording in 1962 as one of the finest classical records of the year. The article, emphasizing Benson's "amazing dynamic shadings and nuances of touch," effectively launched her international concert career as a clavichordist and fortepianist. Benson was the first in America to play music from various fifteenth-century tablatures and to perform eighteenth-century free fantasies of Carl Philipp Emanuel Bach. Her fortepiano repertoire extended from Haydn and Mozart to John Field and Fanny Mendelssohn.

Benson was a pioneer not only as an artist and teacher but also as a researcher, studying and performing on historical keyboard clavichords and fortepianos in all the great museum collections of the world. She has shared her expertise with numerous instrument makers through the years, helping them to understand the rich subtleties and delicate beauties of the great historic keyboards and to bring them to life in modern realizations.

In her tours of the Middle East and Asia, Benson took time to seek out the music of these countries. Her experiences in old Lebanon and Syria, for example, overlapped with those of Tom Binkley in the Middle East. From the ecstatic singing of Egypt's Om Kulthum to the distant sounds of the rebaba played by a nomad, she experienced what "ornamentation" and "improvisation" as a natural part of music might mean.

Joan Benson's advocacy of modern Western music led her to Olivier Messiaen's class at the Paris Conservatoire, to the University of Utrecht Institute of Sonology, and to Stanford's Center for Computer Research in Music and Acoustics. She has performed works for both clavichord and piano by such modern composers as John Cage, David Loeb, Lou Harrison, and Chris Chafe. Benson's recent publications include articles in *Clavichord International* (November 2006) and *De Clavicordio I* (1994), *De Clavicordio VI* (2004), and *De Clavicordio VIII* (2008).

In 2007 Joan Benson gave a two-week clavichord workshop at Indiana University that inspired a DVD of her ideas and this handbook. This duo offers important beginning exercises and lessons for the potential clavichordist. They also provide a vibrant portrait of a clavichord pioneer who takes us from sixteenth-century keyboard masters to the frontiers of electronic music research.

Sample of Joan Benson's Concert Venues

This list is ordered by location. In addition, Benson has performed at most of the major universities throughout the United States.

Baltimore, Maryland, Evergreen Concert Series, Johns Hopkins University

Beirut, Lebanon, American University

Berlin, Musikinstrumenten Museum

Boston, Massachusetts, Museum of Fine Arts

Brussels, Belgium, Musée des Instruments de Musique

Carmel, California, Bach Festival

Cleveland, Ohio, Museum of Art Concert Series

Copenhagen, Denmark, Carl Claudius Collection

Delft, Holland, Prinzenhof

Findhorn, Scotland, International Spring Festival

Geneva, Switzerland, Conservatoire de Musique

Geneva, Switzerland, Musée d'Instruments Anciens de Musique

Great Barrington, Massachusetts, Aston Magna Summer Festival

Hong Kong, Cultural Centre Concert Series and
    Chinese University of Hong Kong

Indonesia, National Television

London, Royal College of Music

London, Victoria and Albert Museum

Magnano, Italy, Musica Antica a Magnano,
    International Clavichord Symposiums

Minneapolis, Minnesota, Walker Art Gallery

Munich, Ludwig-Maximilians-Universität and Hochschule für Musik

New Haven, Connecticut, Yale Collection of Musical Instruments

New York City, Italian Embassy
New York City, Mannes School of Music
New York City, Metropolitan Museum of Art
New York City, Music before 1800 Concert Series
New York City and Pittsburgh, Frick Museums
New York State, Pepsico International Summerfare
New Zealand, concerts in Auckland, Wellington, and Christchurch
Paris, Bibliothèque Nationale de France
Paris, Conservatoire National Supérieur de Musique
Paris, Rothschild Palace
San Francisco, De Young Museum
Stockholm, Sweden, Musikmuseet
Vienna, Austria, Habsburg Palace
Vienna, Austria, Haydn's Home, Celebration for
    250th Anniversary of Haydn's Birth
Washington, D.C., Folger Library
Washington, D.C., Smithsonian Institution
William Kapell International Piano Festival and Competition, Clarice
    Smith Performing Arts Center, College Park, Maryland
Woodstock, New York, Zen Mountain Monastery and Art Center

Reviews

Benson has been praised for unusually sensitive and stylish interpretations in concert and on recordings of a repertory that spans keyboard music from the Renaissance to the Viennese Classics and includes also contemporary works, some of which were written for her. Her work has been crucial in the revival of interest in the fortepiano and the music of C. P. E. Bach.

Howard Schott, in *The New Grove Dictionary of American Music*

The most unusual of the week's debut recitals was that of Joan Benson last Sunday afternoon at the Frick Collection. It was unusual partly because the Frick rarely solicits news coverage of its concerts, given their popularity and the small room in which they transpire, but mostly because Miss Benson is such a distinctive artist. . . . But the clavichord is an almost astonishingly intimate instrument, barely audible at pianissimo. . . . It is thus the ideal vehicle for poetic subtleties of expression, and Miss Benson seemed its ideal interpreter.

John Rockwell, *New York Times*

She completely fulfills C. P. E. Bach's *The True Art of Keyboard Playing*. She declaimed so clearly and shaped the tones in such a diversified way that each *Affekt* (mood) found its perfect expression. Joan Benson's art of rubato and her way of improvisation gave a masterful interpretation to the violently emotional Fantasia in C minor, a peak in clavichord literature.

Südwest-Presse, Germany

Imagination, fingers and sound are a continuum of musical experience. She does not seem so much to coax the sounds from the strings as to magically breathe life into the latent music.

Evening Post, Wellington, New Zealand

Her performance was lifted to a level of perfection by her clear phrasing, lively rhythm, and all the power of musical accentuation possible on this delicate instrument.

Politiken, Copenhagen, Denmark

Joan Benson has developed a highly sensitive way of performing. . . . She shows complete mastery of the limited inflections possible on "touched" strings.

Allgemeine Zeitung, Frankfurt, Germany

Benson is a superb musician with an unusual sense of proportion, phrasing and those tiny points of playing that make a true artist. . . . Not only her playing but her programming reveals a strong and vivid personality.

San Francisco Chronicle

C. P. E. Bach is a composer whose works display in a unique way the element of fantasy in music. Joan Benson is uniquely gifted with a fantasy equal to that of the Bach son. Her interpretations of his works are immutable, a rare experience for the listener. At the basis of her playing is a control born of a solid comprehension of the essence of the music, upon which she bases the freest possible and most expressive performance. Her playing is to be sought after, for there is nothing like it.

Professor William Mahrt, Stanford University

Notes

1. Clavichord for All Keyboardists

1. For information on early pianos, see Coles, *The Pianoforte in the Classical Era;* Harding, *The Piano-Forte* (for excellent drawings of the action); Good, *Giraffes, Black Dragons, and Other Pianos;* and Pollens, *The Early Pianoforte.*
2. See Kottick, *Early Keyboard Instruments.*
3. Mason, *Memories of a Musical Life,* 18.
4. David and Mendel, *The New Bach Reader,* 334–35.
5. Bach, *Geistliche Gesäng nach Christoph Christian Sturm.*

2. Preparing to Play

1. Benson, "Qigong for Pianists."
2. C. P. E. Bach, *Essay,* 42–43.

4. Clavichord Lessons, Series II

1. Türk, *School of Clavier Playing,* 133. Also see Bach, *Essay,* 44–47.

5. Preparing for Pieces

1. Bach, *Essay,* 101. For Emanuel Bach's complete text on the trill, see 99–112.
2. Ibid., 101.
3. For Türk's complete text on the trill, see his *School of Clavier Playing,* 245–64.
4. Ibid., 29.
5. Bach, *Essay,* 110.
6. Ibid., 101.
7. Ibid.
8. For the term "suffix," see ibid., 103.
9. Ibid., 104.
10. For more details, see ibid., 127–32.
11. Ibid., 129.
12. Ibid., 87.
13. Türk, *School of Clavier Playing,* 281.
14. Bach, *Essay,* 156.
15. Burney, *The Present State of Music,* 269–70.
16. Bach, *Essay,* 81.
17. Ibid., 82.

7. Exploring the Past

1. Apel, *The History of Keyboard Music;* and Silbiger, *Keyboard Music.*
2. See Kosner, "Arnaut de Zwolle"; Huber, "The Clavichord," 5–12.
3. Ripin, "The Early Clavichord."
4. See Wallner, *Das Buxheimer Orgelbuch.*
5. Soderlund, *How Did They Play?,* 23. This well-documented book has been useful for my research because it gives a detailed overview of keyboard technique from the fifteenth through the nineteenth centuries.
6. Rodgers, "Early Keyboard Fingering," 172. Consult also the section on Buchner (7–14) and the facsimile and translation of *Fundamentum* (172–80).
7. Ibid., 8–9.
8. For the entire piece, see Soderlund, *How Did They Play?,* 24.
9. Keyboard transcriptions of some of Isaac's vocal pieces are included in Amerbach, *Die Tabulaturen.*
10. Ibid., 8.
11. Picker, "Henry Bredemers."
12. Brauchli, *The Clavichord,* 52.
13. Ibid., fig. 316.
14. Ibid., fig. 3.17, or on the cover, in color.
15. Ferer, *Music and Ceremony.*
16. See Ferer, "The Capilla Flamenca."
17. See Cabezón, *Collected Works.*
18. For a picture of this technique, see Brauchli, *The Clavichord,* 74.
19. Rodgers, "Early Keyboard Fingering," 229.
20. Santa María, *The Art of Playing the Fantasia,* 118–20.
21. See Hogwood, "The Clavichord."
22. See Adlam, "An English Repertoire."
23. See Soderlund, *How Did They Play?,* 50.
24. Ibid.
25. See Attaignant, *Transcriptions.*
26. See Chambonnières, *Oeuvres complètes.*
27. Froberger, *New Edition,* IV.1:22.
28. Ibid., IV.1:xxxvii.
29. Bach, *The Letters,* 72.
30. Fischer, *Sämtliche Werke,* 12.
31. For the short octave, C is on E, D on F♯, E on G♯, with F in its normal place. Sometimes F♯ and G♯ keys are divided in half so that F♯ contains D and F♯, and G♯ contains E and G♯.
32. Fischer, dedication to *Blumen-Büschlein,* in *Sämtliche Werke.*

8. Exploring Eighteenth-Century Germany

1. Butt, "Bach's Metaphysics," 52.
2. Forkel, *On Johann Sebastian Bach's Life,* 436.

3. Stauffer, "Changing Issues," 218.

4. Little and Jenne, *Dance,* 14.

5. See Hilton, *Dance and Music.*

6. Bach and Agricola, Obituary of J. S. Bach.

7. Türk, *School,* 146.

8. For further information on J. S. Bach, see David and Mendel, *The New Bach Reader;* Troeger, *Playing Bach;* and Butt, *The Cambridge Companion.*

9. Burney, *The Present State,* 2:269–70.

10. Johann Joachim Quantz, flute virtuoso, Frederick the Great's teacher, and Emanuel Bach's colleague, wrote *Versuch einer Anweisung die Flöte traversiere zu spielen* (*On Playing the Transverse Flute*), first published in 1752.

11. Bach, open letter published in the *Hamburger unpartheischer Correspondent,* 1773, in *Essay,* 4.

12. Bach, *Essay,* 147.

13. Ibid., 52.

14. Ibid., 153.

15. Ibid., 41–78. (It is important to have read the entire book.)

16. Ibid., 58.

17. Ibid., 57.

18. Isolated cases include *La Philippine* (1755), the undated Allegretto in F (Wq 116/19), and the Allegro in D (Wq 116/20). More important are his two volumes of *Short and Easy Clavier Pieces for Beginners, with Varied Repeats and Added Fingerings* (Wq 113 and 114), published in 1766 and 1768. See C. P. E. Bach, *The Complete Works,* Series 1, *Keyboard Music.*

19. Türk, *School,* 19.

20. Ibid., xiv.

21. Ibid., 19.

22. Ibid., 13.

23. Ibid., 20.

24. Ibid., 129.

25. Ibid.

26. Ibid., 142.

27. Ibid., 135–36.

28. Ibid., 359.

29. Ibid., reworded paraphrase, 337.

30. Ibid., quoting Johann Georg Sulzer, 355.

9. Exploring the Present and Future

1. See Santa María, *The Art of Playing the Fantasia* (*Libro llamado Arte de tañer Fantasia*).

2. Both volume 1 (1753) and volume 2 (1762) are essential for all clavichordists.

3. Bach, *Essay,* 152.

Selected Bibliography

Books and Articles

Adlam, Derek. "An English Repertoire for a Sixteenth Century Clavichord." In *De Clavicordio VI,* edited by Bernard Brauchli, Alberto Galazzo, and Ivan Moody. Proceedings of the International Clavichord Symposium, Magnano, 10–13 September 2003.

Apel, Willi. *The History of Keyboard Music to 1700.* Translated by Hans Tischler. 1972; Bloomington: Indiana University Press, 1997.

Bach, Carl Philipp Emanuel. *Essay on the True Art of Playing Keyboard Instruments.* Translated by William J. Mitchell. New York: W. W. Norton, 1949.

———. *The Letters of C. P. E. Bach.* Translated and edited by Stephen L. Clark. Oxford: Clarendon Press, 1997.

———. *Versuch über die wahre Art das Clavier zu spielen.* Part 1, Berlin: Christian Friedrich Henning, 1753. Part 2, Berlin: Georg Ludewig Winter, 1762.

Bach, Carl Philipp Emanuel, and Johann J. F. Agricola. Obituary of J. S. Bach, 1750, published in 1754. In David and Mendel, *The New Bach Reader,* 306.

Badura-Skoda, Paul. *Edwin Fischer, Meisterkurs in Luzern 1954.* Düsseldorf: Staccato Verlag, 2011.

Bavington, Peter. *Clavichord Tuning and Maintenance.* London: Keyword Press, 2007.

Bedford, Frances. *Harpsichord and Clavichord Music of the Twentieth Century.* Berkeley: Fallen Leaf Press, 1993.

Benson, Joan. "The Clavichord in 20th-Century America." In *Livro de Homenagen a Macario Santiago Kastner,* 143–49. Lisbon: Serviço de Música, 1992.

———. "Clavichord Technique in the Mid-Twentieth Century." In *De Clavicordio I,* 255–57. Proceedings of the International Clavichord Symposium, Magnano, September 1993. Piemonte: Instituto per I Beni Musicali in Piemonte, September 1994.

———. "Piano to Clavichord." *Clavichord International* 10, no. 2 (2006): 38–41.

———. "Qigong for Pianists." *Piano and Keyboard,* September–October 1998, 48–52.

———. "Studying with Macario Kastner a Half-Century Ago." In *De Clavicordio VIII,* edited by Bernard Brauchli, Alberto Galazzo, and Judith Wardman, 59–62. Proceedings of the International Clavichord Symposium, Magnano, 5–8 September 2008.

Brauchli, Bernard. *The Clavichord.* Cambridge: Cambridge University Press, 1998. Paperback edition by John Butt and Laurence Dreyfus. Cambridge: Cambridge University Press, 2005.

Burney, Charles. *The Present State of Music in Germany, the Netherlands and United Provinces.* London: Becket, 1775. Facsimile edition. New York: Broude Brothers, 1969.

Butt, John. *Bach Interpretation: Articulation Marks in Primary Sources of J. S. Bach.* New York: Cambridge University Press, 1990.

———. "Bach's Metaphysics of Music." In Butt, *The Cambridge Companion to Bach,* 46–59.

———, ed. *The Cambridge Companion to Bach.* Cambridge: Cambridge University Press, 1997.

Coles, Michael. *The Pianoforte in the Classical Era.* Oxford: Oxford University Press, 1998.

Couperin, François. *The Art of Playing the Harpsichord.* Edited by Anna Linde. Translated by Mevanwy Roberts. Wiesbaden: Breitkopf & Härtel, 1933.

———. *L'art de toucher le clavecin.* Paris, 1717. Facsimile edition. New York: Broude Brothers, 1979.

David, Hans T., and Arthur Mendel, eds. *The New Bach Reader.* Revised and enlarged by Christoph Wolff. New York: W. W. Norton, 1998.

Diruta, Girolamo. *Il Transilvano* (1593, reprinted in 1597, 1612, and 1625). Facsimile reprints of 1st edition, parts 1 and 2. Bologna: Forni, 1978.

———. *Il Transilvano.* Facsimile edition of parts 1 (1593) and 2 (1609). Annotations and translations into English by Murray C. Bradshaw and Edward J. Soehnien. The Netherlands: Fritz Knuf, 1983; Henryville, Pa.: Institute of Mediaeval Music, 1984.

Elliot, J. H. *Imperial Spain, 1469–1716.* London: Penguin, 2002.

Ferer, Mary Tiffany. *Music and Ceremony at the Court of Charles V: The Capilla Flamenca and the Art of Political Promotion.* Rochester, N.Y.: Boydell Press, 2012.

Forkel, Johann Nikolaus. *Johann Sebastian Bach.* Leipzig: Hoffmeister und Rühnel, 1802.

———. *On Johann Sebastian Bach's Life, Genius, and Works.* In David and Mendel, *The New Bach Reader.*

Harding, Rosamund. *The Piano-Forte.* New York: Da Capo Press Music Reprint Series, 1973.

Helm, E. Eugene. "The 'Hamlet' Fantasy and the Literary Element in C. P. E. Bach's Music." *Musical Quarterly* 58, no. 2 (1972): 277–96.

———. *Music at the Court of Frederick the Great.* Norman: University of Oklahoma Press, 1960.

Hilton, Wendy. *Dance and Music of Court and Theater: Selected Writings of Wendy Hilton.* Hillsdale, N.Y.: Pendragon Press, 1997.

Hitchcock, H. Wiley, and Stanley Sadie, eds. *The New Grove Dictionary of American Music and Musicians.* London: Macmillan Press, 1986.

Hogwood, Christopher. "The Clavichord and Its Repertoire in France and England before 1700." In *De Clavicordio VI,* edited by Bernard Brauchli, Alberto Galazzo, and Ivan Moody. Proceedings of the International Clavichord Symposium, Magnano, 10–13 September 2003.

———. "A Repertoire for the Clavichord. (Including a Brief History of *Bebung*)." In *De Clavicordio II,* edited by Bernard Brauchli, Susan Brauchli, and Alberto Galazzo. Proceedings of the International Clavichord Symposium, Magnano, 21–23 September 1995.

Huber, Alfons, ed. *The Austrian Harpsichord.* Tutzing: Hans Schneider, 2001.

Huber, Alfons. "The Clavichord of Henri-Arnout de Zwolle: Practical Experience with a Reconstruction." *Clavichord International* 9, no. 1 (May 2005): 5–12.

Knights, Francis. "Some Observations on the Clavichord in France." *Galpin Society Journal* 44 (1991): 71–76.

Koster, John. "Arnaut de Zwolle, Henri." In *Grove Music Online,* edited by L. Macy.

Kottick, Edward L. *Early Keyboard Instruments in European Museums.* Bloomington: Indiana University Press, 1997.

Little, Meredith, and Natalie Jenne. *Dance and the Music of J. S. Bach.* Expanded edition. Bloomington: Indiana University Press, 2001.

Mason, William. *Memories of a Musical Life.* New York: Century Company, 1901.

Mersenne, Marin. *Harmonie universelle.* Paris, 1636. Facsimile edition. Paris: Centre National de la Recherche Scientifique, 1986.

Picker, Martin. "Henry Bredemers." In *Grove Music Online,* edited by L. Macy.

Picker, Martin, and Barton Hudson. "Habsburg, 3: Music under the Spanish Habsburgs." In *The New Grove Dictionary of Music,* edited by Stanley Sadie, 8:13–14. New York: Oxford University Press, 1980.

Quantz, Johann Joachim. *On Playing the Transverse Flute.* Translated by Edward R. Reilly. London: Faber and Faber, 1985. 2nd edition, Boston: Northeastern University Press, 2001.

———. *Versuch einer Anweisung die Flöte traversiere zu spielen.* Berlin: Johann Friedrich Voss, 1752.

Rameau, Jean-Philippe. *Treatise on Harmony.* Translated by Philip Gossett. New York: Dover Publications, 1971.

Reichardt, Johann Friedrich. *Briefe eines aufmerksamen Reisenden die Musik betreffend.* 2 vols. Frankfurt and Leipzig, 1774, 1776.

Ripin, Edwin. "The Early Clavichord." *Musical Quarterly,* 518–38. New York: G. Schirmer, 1967.

———. *Keyboard Instruments: Studies in Keyboard Organology, 1500–1800.* Edinburgh: Edinburgh University Press, 1971.

Ripin, Edwin M., et al. *Early Keyboard Instruments.* The Grove Musical Instrument Series. New York: W. W. Norton, 1989.

Rodgers, Julane. "Early Keyboard Fingering, ca. 1520–1620." Ph.D. dissertation, University of Oregon Graduate School, 1971.

Sadie, Stanley, ed. *The New Grove Dictionary of Music and Musicians.* Oxford: Oxford University Press, 2001.

Saint-Lambert, Monsieur de. *Principles of the Harpsichord.* Translated and edited by Rebecca Harris-Warrick. Cambridge: Cambridge University Press, 1984.

Santa Maria, Fray Tomás de. *The Art of Playing the Fantasia.* Translated by Almonte C. Howell, Jr., and Warren E. Hultberg. Pittsburgh: Latin American Literary Review Press, 1991.

———. *Libro llamado Arte de tāner Fantasia, assi para Tecla como para Vihuela.* Valladolid, 1565. Facsimile edition, Geneva: Minkoff Reprint, 1973.

Schulenberg, David. *The Music of Wilhelm Friedemann Bach.* Rochester, N.Y.: University of Rochester Press, 2010.

Silbiger, Alexander, ed. *Keyboard Music before 1700.* 2nd edition. New York: Routledge, 2004.

Simmonds, Paul. *Workbook for the Eighteenth-Century Clavichord.* Raleigh, N.C.: Lulu Press, 2013.

Smith, Anne. *The Performance of Sixteenth-Century Music.* Oxford: Oxford University Press, 2011.

Soderlund, Sandra. *How Did They Play? How Did They Teach? A History of Keyboard Technique.* Chapel Hill, N.C.: Hinshaw Music, 2006.

Stauffer, George B. "Changing Issues of Performance Practice." In Butt, *Cambridge Companion to Bach,* 218.

Steiner, Thomas Friedemann. "Clavichords No. 2 and 3 in the Leipzig Collection—Some Complementary Thoughts about Their Origins." In *De Clavicordio I,* edited by Bernard Brauchli, Susan Brauchli, and Alberto Galazzo. Proceedings of the International Clavichord Symposium, Magnano, 1993.

Troeger, Richard. *Playing Bach on the Keyboard: A Practical Guide.* Cambridge: Amadeus Press, 2003.

———. *Technique and Interpretation on the Harpsichord and Clavichord.* Bloomington: Indiana University Press, 1987.

Türk, Daniel Gottlob. *Klavierschule, oder Anweisung zum Klavierspielen für Lehrer und Lernende, mit kritischen Anmerkungen.* Leipzig and Halle: Schwickert; Hemmerde und Schwetschte, 1789. Facsimile edition by Erwin R. Jacobi. Basel: Bärenreiter, 1962.

———. *School of Clavier Playing: or, Instructions in Playing the Clavier for Teachers and Students.* Translated and with an introduction and notes by Raymond H. Haggh. Lincoln: University of Nebraska Press, 1982.

Vermeij, Koen. *A Short History of the Clavichord.* Aerdenhout: Clavichord International Press, 2010.

Virdung, Sebastian. *Musica getutscht und ausgezogen* (1511). Translated and edited by Beth Bullard. Cambridge Musical Texts and Monographs. Cambridge: Cambridge University Press, 1993.

Williams, Peter. *J. S. Bach: A Life in Music.* Cambridge: Cambridge University Press, 2007.

Book Series and Periodicals

British Clavichord Society Newsletter
Clavichord International. Published by Het Nederlands Clavichord Genootschap.

De Clavicordio. Proceedings of the International Clavichord Symposium. Magnano, Italy. Biennial volumes, 1993–present.

Galpin Society Journal

Tangents: The Bulletin of the Boston Clavichord Society

Music Editions

Amerbach, Bonifacius. *Die Tabulaturen aus dem Besitz des Basler Humanisten Bonifacius Amerbach.* Tabulaturen des XVI. Jahrhunderts 1. Edited by Hans Joachim Marx. Basel: Bärenreiter Verlag, 1967.

Anthology of Eighteenth-Century Spanish Keyboard Music for Organ, Piano, Harpsichord, or Clavichord. Edited by Suzanne Skyrm, with assistance from Calvert Johnson and John Koster. Colfax, N.C.: Wayne Leupold Edition, 2010.

Attaignant, Pierre. *Transcriptions of Chansons for Keyboard.* Edited by Albert Seay. Corpus Mensurabilis Musicae 20. American Institute of Musicology, 1961.

Bach, Carl Philipp Emanuel. *Achtzehn Probe-Stücke in Sechs Sonaten,* Wq 63, nos. 1–6, for Bach's *Essay* (1753), and *Sechs neue Clavier-Stücke,* Wq 63, nos. 7–12, published in 1787 to accompany the expanded 3rd edition of the *Essay. The Complete Works,* series I, volume 3, *"Probestücke," "Leichte" and "Damen" Sonatas.* Edited by David Schulenberg. Los Altos, Calif.: Packard Humanities Institute, 2005.

———. *The Collected Works for Solo Keyboard.* Facsimile edition, 6 volumes. Edited by Darrell Berg. New York: Garland Publishing, 1985.

———. *Geistliche Gesänge nach Christoph Christian Sturm.* Volumes 1 and 2. Hamburg, 1781. Edited by Ludger Rémy. Dresden: Edition Walhall, 2000.

———. *Kurze und leichte Clavierstücke* (*Short and Easy Clavier Pieces for Beginners, with Varied Repeats and Added Fingerings*), Wq 113 and 114, published in 1766 and 1768. *The Complete Works,* series I, volume 8.1, *Miscellaneous Keyboard Works I.* Edited by Peter Wollny. Los Altos, Calif.: Packard Humanities Institute, 2006.

———. *Sämtliche Klavierwerke.* Edited by Miklos Spanyi. Budapest: Könemann Music Budapest, 1999.

Bach, Johann Sebastian. *Clavier-Büchlein vor Wilhelm Friedemann Bach.* Edited in facsimile by Ralph Kirkpatrick. New Haven, Conn.: Yale University Press, 1959.

———. *Klavierbüchlein für Anna Magdalena Bach 1725.* Facsimile with notes by Gerog von Dadelsen. Kassel: Bärenreiter, 1988.

Bach, Wilhelm. *Friedemann Bach. Piano Music I, Collected Works 1.* Edited by Peter Wollny. Chicago: Carus Publishing, 2009.

Buchner, Johannes. *Orgelwerke.* Edited by Jost Harro Schmidt. Frankfurt: Henry Litolff Verlag, 1974. New York: C. F. Peters, 1982.

Cabezón, Antonio de. *Collected Works for Organ or Other Keyboards.* 5 volumes. Edited by Felipe Petrell. New edition with corrections by Higinio Angelés. Boca Raton, Fla.: Master Music Publications, 1991.

———. *Selected Works for Keyboard Instruments.* Edited by Gerhard Doderer and Miguel Bernal Ripoll. Vol. 1–4. Kassel: Bärenreiter Verlag, 2010.

————. *Works of Music for Keyboard, Harp, and Vihuela: A Compendium of Music. Vol. 2 For Keyboard.* Edited by Paola Erdas. Bologna: Orpheus Ediziona, 2011.

Chambonnières, Jacques Champion de. *Oeuvres complètes.* Translated by Denise Restout. Edited by Paul Brunold and André Tessier. New York: Broude Brothers, 1967.

Couperin, François. *Complete Keyboard Works.* First published in 1888. Edited by Johannes Brahms and Friedrich Chrysander. New York: Dover Publications, 1988.

Fischer, Johann Kaspar Ferdinand. *Sämtliche Werke für Klavier und Orgel.* Edited by Ernst V. Werra. New York: Broude Brothers, 1965.

Fitzwilliam Virginal Book. Edited by J. A. Fuller-Maitland and W. Barclay Squire. Revised edition. New York: Dover Publications, 1979.

Froberger, Johann Jakob. *New Edition of the Complete Keyboard and Organ Works,* volumes III and IV.1. Edited by Siegbert Rampe. New York: Bärenreiter, 2003.

Hässler, Johann Wilhelm. *50 Pièces à l'usage des commencants,* op. 38.

Howells, Herbert. *Howell's Clavichord.* Seven Oaks, Kent: Novello, 1961.

Loeb, David. "For Shinobue and Clavichord." Dedicated to Joan Benson. Manuscript.

Priscilla Bunbury's Virginal Book. Translated and edited by Virginia Brookes. Albany, Calif.: PRB Productions, 1993.

Türk, Daniel Gottlob. *Handstücken für angehende Klavierspieler.* Edited by Cornelia Auerbach. Kassel: Nagels Verlag, 1932. New York: Bärenreiter, 1960.

Wallner, Bertha Antonia, ed. *Das Buxheimer Orgelbuch.* New York: Bärenreiter, 1958.

Extended Bibliography

Ahlgrimm, Isolde. *Manuale der Orgel und Cembalotechnik.* Translated by Eugene Hartzell. Vienna: Ludwig Doblinger, 1982.

Ammerbach, Elias Nicolaus. *Orgel oder Instrument Tabulatur.* Translated by Charles Jacobs. Oxford: Oxford University Press, 1984.

Auerbach, Cornelia. *Die deutsche Clavichordkunst des 18. Jahrhunderts.* Kassel: Bärenreiter, 1959.

Badura-Skoda, Paul. *Interpreting Bach at the Keyboard.* Translated by Alfred Clayton. Oxford: Clarendon Press, 1993.

Baines, Anthony. *Musical Instruments through the Ages.* Harmondsworth: Penguin, 1961.

Barford, Philip. *The Keyboard Music of C. P. E. Bach.* New York: October House, 1965.

Benson, Joan. "Clavichord Perspectives from Goethe to Pound." In *De Clavicordio VI,* 139–47. Proceedings of the International Clavichord Symposium, Magnano, September 2003.

———. "The Effect of Clavichord Technique on the Fortepiano." In *Internationaler Joseph Haydn Kongress Wien 1982.* Munich: G. Henle Verlag, 1986.

Bermudo, Juan. *Declaratión de instrumentos musicales.* Ossuna: Juan de León, 1555.

Boalch, Donald H. *Makers of the Harpsichord and Clavichord 1440–1840.* Oxford: Clarendon Press, 1974. 3rd edition by Andreas H. Roth and Charles Mould, 1995. Version 4, uploaded in 2009, is currently available in PDF format.

Bowles, Edmund A. "A Checklist of Fifteenth-Century Representations of Stringed Keyboard Instruments." In *Keyboard Instruments: Studies in Keyboard Organology,* edited by Edwin M. Ripin. Edinburgh: Edinburgh University Press, 1971. Revised and reprinted, New York: Dover Publications, 1978.

Brauchli, Bernard. "Aspects of Early Keyboard Technique: Hand and Finger Positions as Seen in Early Treatises and Iconographical Documents." *Journal of the American Musical Instrument Society* 18 (1992): 62–102.

Brossard, Sebastian de. *Dictionnaire de musique.* Paris: Ballard, 1703.

Brown, A. Peter. *Joseph Haydn's Keyboard Music: Sources and Style.* Bloomington: Indiana University Press, 1986.

Chanel, Phillippe. "The Clavichord as a Guide to the Interpretation of 15th- to 17th-Century Keyboard Literature." *Diapason* 83, no. 5 (1992): 12–13.

Clark, Stephen L., ed. *C. P. E. Bach Studies.* Oxford: Clarendon Press, 1988.

Cooper, Kenneth. *The Clavichord in the Eighteenth Century.* Ph.D. dissertation, Columbia University, 1971. Ann Arbor, Mich.: University Microfilms International, 1977.

Davison, Archibald T., and Willi Apel. *Historical Anthology of Music.* Cambridge, Mass.: Harvard University Press, 1954.

Dolmetsch, Arnold. *The Interpretation of the Music of the Seventeenth and Eighteenth Centuries.* London, 1915. Introduction by R. A. Harman. Seattle: University of Washington Press, 1969.

Donington, Robert. *The Interpretation of Early Music.* Revised and edited. New York: Saint Martin's Press, 1974.

Faulkner, Quentin. *J. S. Bach's Keyboard Technique: A Historical Introduction.* St. Louis: Concordia, 1984.

Ferguson, Howard. *Keyboard Interpretation from the Fourteenth to the Nineteenth Century.* Oxford: Oxford University Press, 1975.

Forkel, Johann Nikolaus. *Über Johann Sebastian Bachs Leben, Kunst und Kunstwerke. Neue unveränderte Ausgabe.* Leipzig: C. F. Peters, 1855.

Frescobaldi, Girolama. *Toccate e partite . . .* Volume 1. Rome: Borboni, 1708.

Gábry, Györky. "Das Reiseklavichord Mozarts." *Studia Musicologica Academiae Scientiarum Hungaricae* 10 (1968): 153–62.

Georgii, Walter. *Klaviermusik.* Berlin: Atlantis Verlag, 1941.

Good, Edwin. *Giraffes, Black Dragons, and Other Pianos.* Stanford, Calif.: Stanford University Press, 2001.

Graber, Kenneth G. "The Life and Works of William Mason (1828–1908)." Ph.D. dissertation, University of Iowa, 1976.

Habsburg, Otto von. *Charles V.* Translated by Michael Ross. New York: Praeger Publishers, 1967.

Hays, Elizabeth Loretta. "F. W. Marpurg's 'Anleitung zum Clavierspielen' (Berlin, 1755) and 'Principes du Clavecin' (Berlin, 1756): Translation and Commentary." Ph.D. dissertation, Stanford University, 1976.

Helenius-Öberg, Eva. *Svenskt Klavikorbygge 1720–1820.* Uppsala: Almqvist and Wiskell International, 1986.

Hilton, Wendy. *Dance of Court and Theatre: The French Noble Style 1690–1725.* Princeton, N.J.: Princeton Book Company, 1981.

Hipkins, Alfred James. *A Description and History of the Pianoforte and of the Older Keyboard Stringed Instruments.* London: Novello, Ewer and Company, 1896.

Hogwood, Christopher, ed. *The Keyboard in Baroque Europe.* Cambridge: Cambridge University Press, 2003.

Hubbard, Frank. *Three Centuries of Harpsichord Making.* Cambridge, Mass.: Harvard University Press, 1974.

Huber, Alfons. "Konstruktionsprinzipien im Clavichordbau." In *"Musik muss man machen": Eine Festgabe für Josef Mertin.* Vienna: Vom Pasqualatihaus, 1994.

James, Philip. *Early Keyboard Instruments.* London: Peter Davies, 1930.

———. "Haydn's Clavichord and a Sonata Manuscript." *Musical Times,* 1 April 1931, 314–16.

Jeans, Susi. "The Pedal Clavichord and Other Practice Instruments of Organists." *Proceedings of the Royal Music Association,* 77th session, 1950–51. Oxford: Oxford University Press. JSTOR 766144.

Jorgensen, Owen. *Tuning the Historical Temperaments by Ear.* Marquette: Northern Michigan University, 1977.

Kastner, Macario Santiago. *Antonio und Hernando de Cabezón.* Tutzing: H. Schneider, 1977.

———. *The Interpretation of 16th and 17th Century Iberian Keyboard Music.* Translated from Spanish by Bernard Brauchli. Stuyvesant, N.Y.: Pendragon Press, 1987.

Kinkeldey, Otto. *Orgel und Klavier in der Musik des 16. Jahrhunderts.* Leipzig: Breitkopf & Härtel, 1910.

Kirkpatrick, Ralph. *Domenico Scarlatti.* New York: Apollo, 1968.

———. "On Playing the Clavichord." *Early Music* 9 (1981): 293–306.

Kirnberger, Johann Philipp. *Die Kunst des reinen Satzes in der Musik.* Berlin: Decker and Hartung, 1776/79. English translation by David Beach and Jurgen Thym. New Haven, Conn.: Yale University Press, 1982.

———. *Recueil d'airs de danse caractéristiques, pour servir de modèle aux jeunes compositeurs et d'exercice à ceux qui touchent du clavecin.* Berlin: Hummel, 1777.

Kottick, Edward L. *A History of the Harpsichord.* Bloomington: Indiana University Press, 2003.

Le Cerf, Georges. "Note sur le clavicorde et le dulce-melos du Ms. Lat. 7295 de la Bibli. Nat. de Paris de Henri Arnault, médecin des Ducs de Bourgogne." *Revue de musicologie* 37, no. 15 (1931): 1–10; 38, no. 15 (1931): 99–105.

Libin, Laurence. "Keyboard Instruments." *Metropolitan Museum of Art Bulletin* 47, no. 1 (Summer 1989).

Löhlein, Georg Simon. *Clavier-Schule oder kurze und gründliche Anweisung zur Melodie und Harmonie, durchgehends mit praktischen Beyspilen erkläret.* Leipzig and Züllichau: Weisenhaus und Frommanischen Buchhandlung, 1765.

Marpurg, Friedrich Wilhelm. *Die Kunst das Clavier zu spielen.* Berlin: Bey Haude und Spener, 1751.

Marshall, Kimberly, ed. *Renaissance 1500–1550.* Volume 9 of *Historical Organ Techniques and Repertoire.* Wayne Leupold Editions, 2004.

Mason, William. *Touch and Technic: Artistic Piano Playing.* Philadelphia: Theodore Presser, 1889.

McGeary, Thomas. "David Tannenberg and the Clavichord in Eighteenth-Century America." *Organ Yearbook* 13 (1982): 94–106.

Milchmayer, Johann Peter. *Die wahre Art, Fortepiano zu spielen.* Dresden, 1787.

Mozart, Leopold. *Versuch einer gründlichen Violinschule.* Augsburg: J. J. Lotter, 1756. English translation by Edith Knocker. London: Oxford University Press, 1948.

Neupert, Hanns. *Das Klavichord.* Kassel: Bärenreiter, 1956.

Ortiz, Diego. *Tratado de glosas . . .* Rome: Dorico and Hermano, 1553. Edited by Max Schneider. Kassel: Bärenreiter, 1936.

Perkins, Leeman L. *Music in the Age of the Renaissance.* New York: W. W. Norton, 1999.

Petri, Johann Samuel. *Anleitung zur practischen Musik vor neuenangehende Sänger und Instrumentspieler.* Lauban: Johann Christoff Wirthgen, 1767.

Pollens, Stewart. *The Early Pianoforte.* Cambridge: Cambridge University Press, 1995.

Praetorius, Michael. Syntagma Musicum, vol. 2, *De Organographia.* Wolfenbüttel, 1619. Translated by Harold Blumenfeld. New York: Bärenreiter, 1949; New York: Da Capo Press, 1980.

Ratner, Leonard. *Classic Music: Expression, Form, and Style.* New York: Schirmer Books, 1980.

Richards, Annette, ed. *C. P. E. Bach Studies.* Cambridge: Cambridge University Press, 2007.

Russell, Raymond. *The Harpsichord and Clavichord: An Introductory Study.* Revised 2nd edition by Howard Schott. New York: Norton, 1973.

Tyler, Royall. *The Emperor Charles the Fifth.* London: George Allen and Unwin, 1956.

Williams, Peter. *The European Organ 1450–1850.* Bloomington: Indiana University Press, 1966.

Wolff, Christoph. *Johann Sebastian Bach: The Learned Musician.* New York: W. W. Norton, 2000.

Zwolle, Arnaut de. *Les traités de Arnaut de Zwolle et de divers anonyms.* Paris: Bibliothèque nationale, MS Latin 7295. Facsimile edition by François Lesure. Kassel: Bärenreiter, 1972.

CD and DVD Contents

CD Track List

1. *Tombeau fait à Paris sur la Mort de Monsieur Blancheroche*
   Johann Jakob Froberger (1616–1667)
   Clavichord by Thomas Goff, England, 1936
   (Repertoire Records, 1962)

2. Free Fantasia in F♯ Minor, Wq 67 (1787)
   Carl Phillip Emanuel Bach (1714–1788)
   Clavichord by Jacobus Verwolf, Holland, 1960
   (Repertoire Records, 1962)

3. Fantasia II in C Major, *für Kenner und Liebhaber,* vol. 5,
      Wq 59/6 (1785)
   C. P. E. Bach
   Pianoforte by John Broadwood and Son, 1795
   (Orion Master Recordings, Giveon Cornfield, 1975)

4. Fantasia in D Minor, K. 397
   Wolfgang Amadeus Mozart (1756–1791)
   Pianoforte by John Broadwood and Son, 1795
   (Recorded by David Wilson, 1982)

5. Sonata in G Minor, Moderato, Hob. XVI/44/2
   Franz Joseph Haydn (1732–1809)
   Clavichord by Johann Christoph Georg Schiedmayer, Germany, 1796
   Boston Museum of Fine Arts
   (Titanic Records, Ralph Dopmeyer, 1980)

6. Fantasie in E Minor, F. 21
   Wilhelm Friedemann Bach (1710–1784)
   Clavichord by Pehr Lindholm, Sweden, 1785
   (Recorded by David Wilson, 1982)

7. Sonata in D Major, Hob. XVI/24
   Franz Joseph Haydn
      Allegro
      Adagio
      Finale: Presto
   Pianoforte by John Broadwood and Son, 1795
   (From live concerts, Smithsonian Institution, 1975,
      and Arch St., Berkeley, 1973)

8. *In a Landscape* (1948)
   John Cage (1912–1992)
   Hamburg Steinway grand piano, 1966
   (From live concert, Music Today's Festival of the Millennium, 2000)

This CD represents four decades of Joan Benson's artistry. It begins with her first clavichord LP, chosen by *Saturday Review* as one of the best classical recordings for 1962. Her revival of C. P. E. Bach's emotional Free Fantasia in F♯ Minor awakened international acclaim.

Joan's sensitive and spontaneous interaction with audiences was an important part of her music making. Hence this CD emphasizes her exquisite interpretations of eighteenth century, free fantasias filled with improvisation-like, quick-changing moods. It also offers, for the first time, recordings of her live performances of music by Haydn and John Cage.

Instruments range from her original Lindholm clavichord to a Hamburg Steinway grand piano. Settings vary from a San Francisco bedroom to a concert hall in Washington, D.C.

Joan Benson's CD was produced by Barry Phillips, (winner of a 2012 Grammy Award for engineering and producing Ravi Shankar's music). Eric Jacobs of Audio Archive and John Nunes made fine digital transfers, along with Jay Kadis and Bill Levey. Phillips carefully reduced or eliminated hiss, clicks, pops, and hums, using Izotope restoration software. Every effort was made to retain the subtle and contrasting dynamics in which Joan Benson excelled.

DVD Contents

1. Introduction
2. Excerpts
3. Flexibility Exercises
4. Clavichord Mechanism
5. Finding Your Voice
6. The Dolmetsch/Chickering Clavichord
7. Student One
8. Student Two
9. Student Three
10. Student Four
11. Student Six
12. Closing Thoughts

Joan Benson has performed throughout the world, garnering the respect of classical music enthusiasts and major contemporary composers. She has taught on the faculty at Stanford University, the University of Oregon, and the Aston Magna Academy in Massachusetts.